RENAISSANCE MANAGEMENT

renaissance MANAGEMENT

the rebirth of energy & innovation in people & organizations

stephen carter

First published in 1999
First published in paperback in 2001

Kogan Page Limited
120 Pentonville Road
London
N1 9JN
UK

Kogan Page Limited
163 Central Avenue, Suite 2
Dover
NH 03820
USA

British Library Cataloguing in Publication Data

A CIP record for this book is available from the British Library.

ISBN 0 7494 3483 X

Typeset by Patrick Armstrong, Book Production Services
Printed and bound by Biddles Ltd, Guildford and King's Lynn

CONTENTS

PREFACE TO THE PAPERBACK EDITION

FROM THE writer's point of view, a book is rarely finished (leading to the ongoing state of anxiety that is the lot of the publisher!). Looking back at the hardback edition of *Renaissance Management*, there are, of course, things that I would probably want to change. Nothing substantive fortunately, I still believe in the central argument of the book – that if organizations wish to flourish in these uncertain times they have to release the potential and individuality of their employees and contributors in order to have the energy and momentum to succeed.

What I see more clearly now than I did at the time of writing is the impact of recognizing individuals as inconsistent and changeable, as proposed by Mike Apter's discoveries about motivation and personality. As well as mapping out how our changeable motivations lead us to seek satisfaction in a variety of ways at work, which therefore drive a range of behaviours that can add enormous value to an organization, Apter's thinking can be taken a stage further. We need to recognize, that because of our changing motivations, that which we perceive as important in a given situation can differ markedly not just between different individuals but also within a particular individual over time. Now if an organization restricts the way an individual can be motivated then it also runs the risk of its contributors not recognizing threats, opportunities, problems etc. Or if they do, seeing them only in a limited way and thereby offering a skewed response to an opportunity or risk that requires a more complex, multi-perspective solution. The challenge is therefore even more urgent for organizations to provide motivationally rich and compelling work environments.

Several people who have read the book have discussed with me what sort of people should lead the changes that would build a more energetic aligned organization. The book argues, I think correctly, that change should happen through an iterative process of local initiatives and strategies rather than a purely top-down approach. To make this powerful and effective, organizations need to develop a cadre of leaders who demonstrate leadership in themselves and release it in others. That is what I have termed a 'community of leaders' who act as an intensive network across the business. Such a community has forged common values and understanding and is capable of intensive open communication, influence, collective action and innovation. It is a leadership group able to work together, collectively and in sub-groups, and is the powerhouse of effective corporate change.

I guess members of such a group will have a certain 'maverick tendency'. Interestingly, Paul Johnson said of the original Renaissance leaders in regard to the Universities – representatives of the orthodoxy – that they were 'outsiders' reacting against institutions, which 'stamped on individualism and innovation'.[1]

The development of such groups will probably require direct intervention and is the subject of much of my work at present. I would be very interested to discuss with anyone else who is tackling such challenges.

Finally, in the list of acknowledgements at the start of the hardback edition of this book, a name was missed out. Christopher Gasson gave me much help in re-casting parts of the initial chapters of the book and I am grateful for the opportunity to express my thanks and put this omission right in print.

1. Johnson, P (2000) *The Renaissance: A short history*, Modern Library Publications, Random House, New York

INTRODUCTION

WHY *RENAISSANCE* MANAGEMENT?

ALTHOUGH the title of this book contains the word 'renaissance', it is not a book about history, but a book about the future. It is a book about people, and how organizations really can make people their most important asset. It is not another theory, or an attempt to outline the 'one best way' discovered by a particular organization or guru. Instead, it tries to fit together the different steps, big and small, that many organizations are taking in order to respond to the challenges they have in common.

There is scarcely an aspect of human existence that is not shaped and influenced by organizations. They are amongst the most complex manifestations of human activity, operating in multi-faceted and multi-layered ways, which can often defy understanding and analysis. In an environment in which the winds of change blow strongly, and from capricious directions, managing these organizations can be a fraught task. For many of them, a re-evaluation of the context, purpose and process of management is long overdue.

Why 'Renaissance Management'?

But first – why 'Renaissance Management'?

The term has been buzzing around my head for a number of years. What I first thought I meant by it has developed quite dramatically. At the start, I used the term to express what I saw as the inevitable growth in multi-skilling required of managers as organizations rid themselves of layers of staff, introduced increasingly sophisticated technology, and searched ever more frantically to reduce fixed overheads and achieve the flexibility that they felt sure was the key to their survival.

In the past, a cynical view of managers would see them as little more than message carriers between the top and bottom of an organization, with some policing and law enforcement thrown in for good measure. Their imperative was control. Managers will now be required to behave in quite different ways. They will often be required to operate with teams of people over whom they do not have direct control. Instead of employing their expertise with their direct reports, they will be asked to utilize it in consultation with other parts of the organization. They will be told – and will surely recognize the irony – that their role is now not to direct people, but to coach and develop. Managers will increasingly be asked to master new skills and develop new levels of expertise within a dynamic set of expectations; that set of expectations will be unique to a particular organization at a particular time. It seems, therefore, that previous fixed notions of what managers do will be of limited value in helping them meet these expectations. A more relevant notion on which to hang this multi-skilled, complex role seemed to be that of the Renaissance Man of history, who was popularly seen as the multi-talented soldier-merchant-poet-artist.

Recognizing the changes that had taken place, I began to look for a description for the modern equivalent (of either gender) within an organization, and to prepare an article on renaissance management. Referring to some history books on the Renaissance, I found surprisingly few references to the multi-talented paragon, but several remarks caught my eye:

instead of setting an ideal before man to be obtained by sacrificing his individuality, it insisted on the further development of the individual character and claimed the freedom to explore possibilities without hindrance it led to a revolt against the absolute standards of the Church.[1] *[For Church read senior management]*

the zest for knowledge, combined with the will to experiment were characteristic...[2]

the Renaissance was an explosion of inquiry and learning.

THE RISE OF THE INDIVIDUAL AND THE RELEASE OF ENERGY

The Renaissance was about the release of energy and learning, and the rise of the individual. It was about curiosity and experimentation and an exploration of the link between art and science. It was also about building upon what had already been learned – with all the pitfalls that implies – and not re-inventing the wheel. This seemed to make many connections, for example, with current notions about the learning organization and the enthusiasm for empowerment. It seemed to sum up the spirit of what I was finding as I worked with different organizations in many different countries, and went far beyond the idea of multi-skilling.

The Renaissance was probably the first people revolution. It did not topple tyrants or bring power to the masses, but it did liberate individuals from a mindset which restricted their aspirations.

In medieval times, Man's place in the world was defined by the feudal hierarchy, and his fate was determined by God. The Renaissance replaced this view with a humanist outlook, which put man at the centre of a universe he controlled. His achievements were celebrated. This led to a blossoming of the arts, and also to an explosion in mercantilism, and the great discoveries of America and the Cape route to the Indies.

Since then, there have been numerous people revolutions in the political sphere, giving everyone a greater say in their future.

A NEW REVOLUTION

Today, another type of people revolution is happening – within organizations. At one time, the place of an individual within an organization was determined by his or her position in the management hierarchy, and the fate of the organization and everyone within it was in the hands of the chief executive. Now, however, organizations are finding that change is pulling apart their structure, forcing them to take more and more account of the talents, differences and personalities of their employees.

At one time, it was possible for an organization to define how people worked, but now it is the other way round. The people in an organization will increasingly define how that organization works. The rate of change in the marketplace means that job descriptions have to be fluid and, to a certain extent, self-created.

This reliance is confusing and stressful for many organizations, but it can also make them great. By freeing people to be themselves, organizations can gain access to the whole contribution they can make – their creativity, their ability to learn and to challenge, and their willingness to support their colleagues – all essential if an organization is to be able to respond to change.

However, this 'Renaissance' is about more than just responding to change. It is also about building lasting competitive advantage. This cannot be achieved by depending on access to capital, nor by lowering labour costs. Organizations have to look to the uniqueness of their people, and to what those people can do to give the organization the edge.

The Renaissance of an Organization

The renaissance of an organization is not a rediscovery of classical values, or a great cultural blossoming, but the rebirth of the original energy of the organization.

Most organizations find that, as they grow, they tend to become too large to be responsive to the market. They find it difficult to adapt quickly to change, and when they are forced to do so, the experience is often so traumatic that it is counter-productive. They also lose their ability to relate to their smallest units – their people.

This renaissance is about rediscovering the values – energy, innovation and responsiveness – of the small business operation, where individuality really counts, without losing the undoubted benefits of size. An organization can achieve these values by allowing itself to be totally defined by the personalities of its members.

This renaissance has already begun in many organizations. Even enormous conglomerates such as General Electric and Asea Brown Boveri are notable examples. They have been among the first to recognize the importance of being big, but acting small. As conglomerates with interests in fast-moving industries, they need to be locally responsive, and focused on individual contribution, while maintaining those benefits, such as institutional expertise, global reach, and access to capital, which go with being big.

Overview of This Book

This book looks at sources of energy at an organizational level through market alignment, and sources of energy at an individual level through a deeper concern for the individuality of employees. It also looks at the structure and processes and climate that will keep these two sources of energy aligned and mutually reinforcing in a virtuous energy cycle.

The book is divided into two sections. The first section is concerned with explaining 'Renaissance Management'. Why can we argue for the rise of the individual, and what do we mean by a high-energy response built out of superior market alignment and individual energy? The second section is concerned with exactly how an organization might work in order to become a successful 'Renaissance Organization'. Chapter 1 provides an overview of a Renaissance approach and what is driving it.

Chapter 2 looks at the issue of the rise of the individual more closely in terms of its market context, exploring why it is a potential organizational response to operating in a volatile, more competitive environment, and how it is driven by the market. This issue has an important impact on the relationship between the individual and the organization. Chapter 3 focuses on what exactly energy might mean in an organizational context, and how an organization can strategically and locally maximize the energy it gains from its relationship to the market. Chapters 4 and 5 are concerned with the other side of the energy cycle – the nature and requirements for a greater individual contribution.

The second section begins with Chapter 6, which deals with the architecture of an organization that would allow for the most productive relationships with a market-place at both local and strategic levels.

Once energy has been created, it is important that it should be used most productively, to drive further innovations and increased levels of responsiveness through continued individual employee commitment. Chapter 7 therefore analyses the basis for energy efficiency within an organization, looking at such features as simple structures, networks, measuring energy, and so on. Most of the arguments in the book up to this point emphasize the need for diversity and autonomy, but Chapter 8 offers a range of strategies for building the connections within an organization, with the aim of establishing integration and alignment without over-control.

By far the most important aspect of modern organizations seems to have been the development of a variety of forms of team working, and the issues surrounding these are explored in Chapters 9 and 10. Finally, Chapters 11 and 12 pull the strands of the book together, looking specifically at how a Renaissance Organization will be managed, and what will be the role of managers themselves within such an organization.

References

1. Thompson, J (1964) *The Achievements of Western Civilisation*, Darton, Longman and Todd, London.
2. Green, V H H (1952) *Renaissance and Reformation*, University Press, Aberdeen.

Part

1

CHAPTER 1

RENAISSANCE MANAGEMENT – AN OVERVIEW

AMONG THE many challenges that face the management of organizations, two of the most important are the volatility of the markets in which they operate and the ever-growing need to deal with customers, employees and other stakeholders as individuals. As will be discussed there is a strong link between the two factors – a link which successful organizations will recognize can be harnessed for ongoing advantage. The development and management of organizations who can respond to this will distinguish them from those who don't – who instead may run the risk of finding themselves locked in a situation of trying to grind out their survival with a disaffected workforce.

The impact of these two forces on those organizations that are exposed to them most completely is visceral and powerful. For many it requires fundamental changes to the way they think and act. Changes that are reflected not only in strategy, structure and processes but also in more subtle areas such as the relationship an individual has with his or her organization and the culture and climate that need to exist.

The level of change can be dramatic – the situation highlighted in Connections, overleaf, is more common than many managers think.

CONNECTIONS: THE RATE OF CHANGE

Over last two years, I have been asking groups of managers from twelve different businesses the following question: 'Think of the job you are in now. How far back in time would you have to go before what you were doing then would be 50 per cent different from what you are doing now, *regardless of any changes in job title*?' The responses, from several hundred managers, were remarkably consistent; the average length of time for a 50 per cent change was 8–10 months.

This data has some interesting implications.

It would be reasonable to argue that a job that is 50 per cent different within 10 months is, in essence, a different job. A number of implications might be drawn from this, in terms of the relationship between organizations and individuals, as follows:

- role specifications and job descriptions will almost certainly be out of date;
- performance targets are unlikely to reflect the job that someone is actually doing;
- there will be an inevitable impact on work teams, and development will have to focus on team joining rather than team development;
- most top-down directions will have been modified and, in some cases, superseded by the time they reach local level.

These are examples of the 'speed of change' that features so frequently in popular management literature, where one piece of change piles upon another, and the cliché 'the only constant is change' holds true. Organizationally, it is important to consider what is driving this level of change. Contrary to popular belief, it is not a half-demented senior team dreaming up pet projects and responding to fashionable ideas. It is, rather, the changing shape of the markets in which organizations operate, and their endeavours, effective and ineffective, to respond to that changing market. The level of volatility within an organization is a reflection of the volatility outside it, and that level of volatility will weed out those organizations which cannot respond and act quickly enough, and are always in a state of catch-up.

Everywhere, it seems, there is a pressure to change, and a sense of fundamental shifts – in the way we are going to live our lives, in the way our markets work, in the way we work, in the way we build our institutions and systems. What type of organization is going to thrive in these circumstances, and how will people work for them and in them? Organizations will be forced to think differently. Many are already doing so, and this book is about what can be learnt from their experiences.

THE CHANGING SHAPE OF ORGANIZATIONS

Organizations reflect the societies and markets in which they operate. As these evolve, so should organizations. Sometimes, however, they get left behind, especially if they continue to operate to a set of assumptions that held good for previous markets.

One of the most fundamental of these traditionally held assumptions is that organizations are about top-down control. In this scenario, senior managers set the strategy, determine the processes, control budgets, and make a vast array of other decisions. They may employ one or two experts to help them with advice and suggestions, but, ultimately, they are in command. Business is executed by hiring others who are very good at doing as they are told.

In the past, there were good reasons for this (see Connections, below). Markets were more stable, offering the opportunity of economies of scale based on a tight, unified approach. In an age of mass production, consistency and efficiency were the most important factors to organizations.

In fact, even in relatively stable times there has always been a level of uncertainty and unpredictability, and a need for responsiveness and change challenging the control of senior management. In addition, there has always been commercial reward for responding to local market differences. However, senior managers, far removed from the action, found the uncertainty, unpredictability and differences difficult to understand, and therefore tried to ignore them.

Successful organizations have, therefore, always had to set against their desire for neat, unified top-down control an opposing need for an element of autonomy, diversity and local responsibility – a touch of inconsistency in a well-ordered organizational world.

CONNECTIONS: THE BIGGER PICTURE

One feature of the twentieth century has been its ability to create vast, all-powerful political and industrial organizations, in which people surrender their individuality and diversity to a common cause and a sense of duty. Within businesses, this was driven by the huge benefits that economies of scale could bring. The key was replication and predictability, and the aim was standardization – in roles, processes, systems or outputs. Control, centralization and integration were held to be the key to success, and this approach has shaped business in the last hundred years or more.

At the same time, within society at large there has been a rise in an opposing force of autonomy and diversity. One expression of this has been the importance of individuality, in terms of choice, rights and potential contribution. This has had an impact on organizations, principally through the power of consumer choice. It has had little impact on the way organizations work, except in those industries where there is a skills shortage, or which demand talents that require individual expression. In developed economies, greater and greater freedoms are strengthening this opposing force.

The importance of inconsistency

Thus until the very recent past it made market sense for most organizations to emphasize the primary forces of control and consistency. Now, things are changing. The rapid developments in technologies and markets, and the changing demographic balance (see Chapter 2) have all toughened the competitive challenge faced by organizations. Competition has demanded increases in productivity and reduced times to market, incredible levels of flexibility and responsiveness, and a continuing demand for innovation.

The result of this is that there is growing pressure within organizations to acknowledge the opposing forces of autonomy and diversity – the forces of inconsistency. This is reflected at management levels by a growing need to allow local managers more freedom to manoeuvre, and to give those in contact with customers the authority to take any action necessary to meet those customers' demands. This growing need is addressed by global companies such as Unilever, who have for a long time recognized the necessity of coupling global brands and innovations with an acknowledgement of and responsiveness to local needs. More recently, they have seen the need to re-create job structures, to make sure that every decision is taken at the appropriate level within the organization, and no higher.

The situation in which many organizations now find themselves might be called the 'consistency/inconsistency dilemma' (see Fig. 1.1).

CONSISTENCY	INCONSISTENCY
Control	Autonomy
Integration	Diversity
Centralization	Localization
Roles	Individuals
Function-led	Customer-led

Fig. 1.1. The consistency/inconsistency dilemma

Every dimension of this dilemma requires an organization to find its own place in response to the market conditions it faces, and its strategic response. However, because the dilemma is essentially paradoxical, the point is dynamic and likely to change. One feature of such a dilemma is that, for various reasons, the further an organization goes in the direction of inconsistency, the less it can depend upon narrow specifications of roles and responsibilities. It will need to encourage flexibility and, at least among certain groups of employees, to adopt an approach that calls upon a more individualistic response.

At one level, these forces will appear in opposition and account for many of the paradoxes of organizational life. At another, when seen in relation to the need for diversity and integration, they lead to the creative tension that drives a flexible and innovative organization, in which individual creativity can lead to organization-wide learning. This is the state of integrated diversity or interdependence. This state has become the keystone objective of many organizations, rather than either of the polarities of dependence or independence. Interdependence means that diversity and autonomous behaviour within the organizations produce a steady supply of innovations, and also that the integrative structures ensure that the whole organization benefits.

Within the terms of this book, the balance between control and autonomy is achieved by establishing a range of processes and techniques, aimed at creating alignment between all the different stakeholders of an organization.

The Balance of Power

The potential here is for a shift in the balance of power. Organizations are no longer able to tell people what to do – people are having to do what the market tells them, rather than what a particular part of the organization expects and predicts. In the organizational body, the brain now needs to be in the feet and the hands, as well as in the head.

Even if reported levels of volatility are largely perceptual, and only partly true, they still change the emphasis. The volatility means that an individual is more than the receiver of a role and a job within an organization but – at least in part – a creator of it. Each individual will have to be prepared creatively to determine his or her contribution, and this requirement will be emphasized by the fact that often he or she will be the only person in a fast-moving environment who can determine the detail of their work. Individuals who contribute in this way will be bringing much more of themselves than the docile employees who complied in the past with accepted roles.

What sort of people are needed to work in such organizations? For a start, they are unlikely to be blindly compliant, working to tightly defined role specifications and job descriptions. The need for 'integrated diversity' makes impossible the Taylorist vision (in which employees fulfil roles carefully defined for them by another) and instead requires a very different sort of individual who is prepared to commit a lot more of him or herself to work.

A Renaissance approach

What are organizations doing to cope better with these levels of change and volatility, and the consequent need to balance more successfully the forces of integration and diversity, consistency and inconsistency, control and autonomy?

It has struck me that organizations which seem to be succeeding appear both to have achieved a great relationship with their marketplaces, expressed as a strong differentiated strategic position through innovation and responsiveness, and a peculiarly high level of focus on individual contribution from staff. One such company is Richer Sounds[1] in the UK, which has the highest sales per square foot of any retail company in the world. Bucking the trend for out-of-town stores, this company sells a huge range of goods alongside hi-fi, focusing on smaller, more intimate stores; their dominance of a market niche gives them a buying power from which customers benefit, through lower prices and value for money. What really gives Richer Sounds its advantage is its outstanding level of customer service. This is achieved through a whole range of innovative and different HR policies, which enable the company to think outside the usual the role/reward/career path structures. (For example, their head of design is a former sales assistant who got bored with selling.)

It seems unlikely that these two factors – brilliantly productive market relationships and focus on individual contribution – are unrelated. Is there any way of characterizing these organizations in order to suggest what the relationship between them might be? (I don't want to be oversimplistic here. I am not suggesting that all strategically differentiated organizations emphasize the individual potential of their staff, nor that organizations that do are necessarily well positioned in their marketplace. I *am* suggesting that organizations that achieve both conditions are well placed to remain successful.)

One approach is to consider what focusing on individual contribution might mean. Treating individuals as individuals, rather than as role holders, implies a much greater expectation of both parties. The organizational view says, 'We need you to contribute, beyond any job description we may try to give you, your energy, enthusiasm, creativity, care – in short, your personality.' The individual view of this relationship says, 'If I am to do this, I want to be treated as an individual with individual needs. I want to be trusted, with information, with decisions, with the integrity and value of my ideas. I want to feel that demands of my life outside work are an issue to which the company wants to respond with flexibility and understanding. I want to grow.'

Meeting the expectations of one party demands much of the other. It takes energy. Individuals can extend the range of their contribution through their motivation and drive, they can offer aspects of themselves that, in the past, they would not even have felt were particularly wanted. This is not a contribution based on hours, but on scope.

In return, an organization will need to expend energy in order to meet the demands of its individuals. Where is that energy to come from?

How will the organization live up to its side of the new, more expansive expectations? It can only come from the organization's relationship with the market-place. If it is locked in a bitter battle for prices and margins to survive, an organization simply will not have the energy to change; what it needs is spare capacity, to allow it to invest in its employees, and its future.

CONNECTIONS: CHANGE

Daryll Conner's book *Managing at the Speed of Change*[2] introduced me to the simple but profound notion of seeing organizations and individuals as having a finite number of 'assimilation points' with which to deal with change. These 'points' are consumed cumulatively by change initiatives within organizations, with the result that minor changes can meet with unforeseen resistance and negative results. Clearly, these 'assimilation points' are another way of conceiving the amount of energy that an organization has available to deal with change. Interestingly, Conner also seems to argue that the basic source of energy in an organization is the 'resilience' of its individuals; the success of the organization will depend on the willingness of the individuals to commit this energy to it. Much of Conner's book is concerned with the process of change management and how to make it more effective. It is also worth considering how organizations can be 'structured' to increase the energy that they have available to deal with change.

Both highly productive market relationships and a focus on individual contribution may be termed high-energy options. To establish and maintain them will require considerable energy investment from an organization, but that organization could reasonably expect a much higher energy return; both options will demand high levels of innovation, flexibility and management time.

It is useful to conceive of the ideal interaction between these two factors as potentially creating a high-energy environment. An organization that achieves this interaction seems to get more energy from its staff, which it can use in all its forms to help it achieve a more productive energy relationship with its market. The energy released may, in turn, liberate more of the energy of the employees through the ability to better acknowledge individual needs. This creates a virtuous energy cycle, in which the differential forms of the energy involved lead to gain for all parties (see Fig. 1.2).

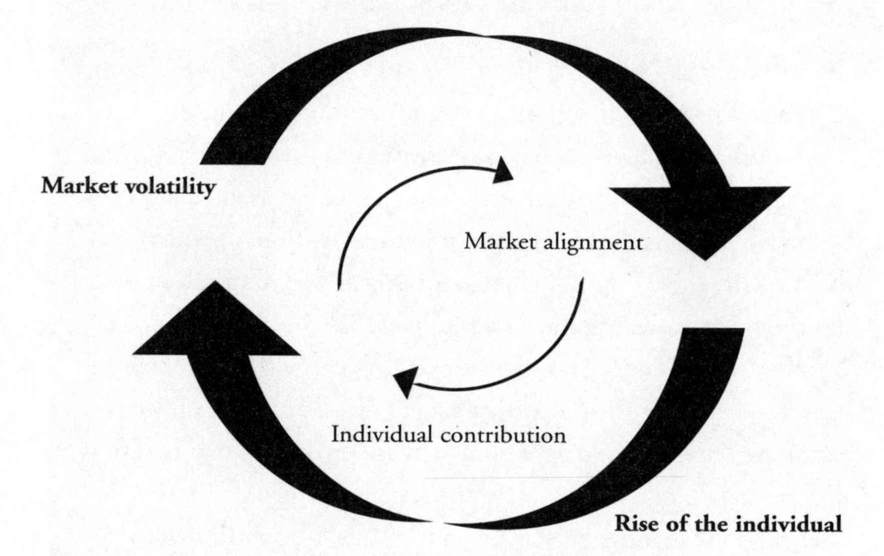

Fig. 1.2. Organizational synergy: the virtuous energy cycle

This idea is similar to the notion of 'organizational slack' – excess resources, above and beyond those required to run an organization on a day-to-day basis, with no view of the future or of any requirement to change or innovate. No organization survives long without spare capacity – very quickly, it is unable to respond to the market-place (for example, over-zealous cost-cutting will immediately bring it down). On the other hand, too much slack is wasteful, and is soon eaten up in pet projects and over-specification. This kind of waste may be avoided by seeing organizational slack as surplus energy, which can, in part, be devoted to creating an organization that is responsive to individual needs.

WHAT IS A 'RENAISSANCE ORGANIZATION'?

Renaissance Management is not a new theory, but a way of looking at what organizations are already doing to help themselves thrive in the twenty-first century. The original Renaissance was about the rise of the individual and developments in learning. The same factors apply to renaissance in organizations – individuality will be an increasing expectation within a workforce, and learning will be a key process. It can also be as much about rediscovering what is already known – organizations simply cannot waste energy re-inventing the wheel. This time, however, the learning will not necessarily come from ancient history, but from the global market-place.

A Renaissance Organization is one that continuously innovates to achieve market alignment through a strategic position that positively differentiates it from its competitors. This allows high-value transactions to take place for the benefit of all the organization's stakeholders. In addition, it commits to establishing a workforce that can fully contribute all the potential of each individual to the benefit of the organization, and of each individual's own success and happiness. Renaissance Management is the approach, in terms of structures, processes, attitudes and beliefs, that helps to build and maintain such an organization.

Establishing a Renaissance Organization is an aspiration, and none of the organizations mentioned in this book perfectly represents the ideal. However, they each hold a piece of the jigsaw of the perfect Renaissance Organization, and have faced the challenge of many of the issues raised in this book.

A NEW RELATIONSHIP

At the heart of this book is the idea that organizations will need to examine closely the basis of the relationship that they have with the individuals who work for them. Central to this is the notion of the psychological contract. Simply, these are the unwritten assumptions that exist between employer and employee about what one can expect from the other. In the past, this was based on the notion of an exchange between long-term job security and compliance to work demands and loyalty. Put more simply: 'I'll give you a job for life if you do exactly as you are told!'

The psychological contract can no longer be based upon this: few employers are in a position to offer long-term job security and, increasingly, employees may not want it (see Chapter 5). In the future, the relationship between employer and employee is more likely to be based on personal development, not on job security. Former UK Secretary of State for Education and Employment Gillian Shephard has said,[3]

> *I suggest that we have to give people a new 'anchor': not security of employment but security of employability. The flexibility and adaptability that people need to be able to change jobs and meet the requirements of employers and the economy can only be provided by life-long learning.*

There is much sense in this proposal. Certainly, the impacts of change driven by technology will almost undoubtedly require continuous development from a workforce and, as organizations change and develop, there will be a far higher degree of mobility between jobs. Given that current estimates suggest that someone entering employment now might expect to have on average seven jobs in his or her working life, the new deal seems a good one; in other words, your current organization will be actively helping you get a job in your next one. More and more organizations seem to be accepting this as a reasonable exchange that will help them to recruit and develop a flexible workforce.

To strengthen the psychological contract, organizations need to examine other hidden clauses that are often not aired. These expectations will include the following:

- being treated with fairness, and involved. Work in the USA on what makes an effective change process has emphasized the need for it to be seen as fair, by creating dialogue and explanation about change.

Individuals need to feel that their views and opinions have been heard, even if those views or opinions are not adopted;
- feeling fulfilled and motivated about the current job, as well as being prepared for the next one;
- being trusted and respected, working in an environment in which the individual can express him or herself without fear or threat.

Additionally, most people would really like to feel inspired and proud of the organization for which they work.

However, exchanging job security alone may not be enough to gain commitment rather than opportunistic compliance from individuals. Commitment is based upon the individual identifying the extent to which he or she is prepared to contribute all aspects of him or herself – energy, intellect and, most of all, what makes them unique. This uniqueness, with all its creative potential, will enrich the resources and ability of an organization to meet the challenges it faces. The currency of this exchange will be as much in terms of emotions as objective rewards, and the skilful handling of this exchange will be vital to an organization's future success.

If these conditions are met, the potential exists to gain real commitment, and a much greater contribution of energy and creativity from individuals by – in the words of one manager I recently met – enabling them 'to bring [their] personality to work'.

The challenge

Organizations are therefore facing a number of related drivers for change, to which they must respond if they are to survive:

- they have to respond to an increasingly competitive and uncertain market-place with brilliant positioning achieved by innovation and responsiveness;
- they have to respond to the fact that their employees will increasingly

need to have the flexibility and motivation to create their own unique contribution;

- they have to find a way of balancing the opposing forces for consistency and inconsistency if they are to maximize their impact in their market-places.

The cleverest organizations will not try to resist this tide of change, but will find the value and potential in it. They will be those organizations that realize that an increasing individual contribution gives them powerful strategic options. It builds responsiveness to market conditions and taps into a reservoir of creativity and energy, and this combination allows for true strategic differentiation.

It is this link between the outer world of market demand and the inner world of motivation and personal action that provides the structure and purpose of this book. The next chapter deals with the drivers of change alluded to here in much more detail. Those readers who are familiar with these issues may wish to skim-read to the final section – 'The energy for managing paradox'.

PROVOCATIONS – THE NEW PSYCHOLOGICAL CONTRACT

The individual's needs

An organization will:

- offer me development, not just for short-term plans but for my long-term career; such development will be not only formal training but also access to projects, tasks and secondments that enhance my portfolio of work experience;
- treat me with justice and provide a working environment that is, and is seen to be, fair;

- provide a working environment in which I find the activities I undertake and the part I play motivating and rewarding;
- ensure that all times in terms of the tasks I undertake and my personal development I receive the feedback I need to deliver the objectives and goals I have.

Organizational needs

Individuals will:

- offer us flexibility and an understanding that work must change and develop, and that this is not a whim of the company, but a necessity of the market;
- offer us loyalty, reflected not in long-term service but in high-energy commitment while working here, and acknowledgement of our needs when you have gone;
- offer us a willingness to learn not just task skills but the skills to deal well with others; so that they are also able to contribute maximally;
- offer us enterprise for the organization and for themselves;
- bring their personality to work.

References

1. Golzen, G (March/April 1998) Richer sounds right, *Human Resources.*
2. Conner, D R (1995) *Managing at the Speed of Change*, Villard Books, New York.
3. Shephard, G, Secretary of State for Employment (November 1996) Keynote Address, Anglo-French colloquium, *The Changing World of Work*, Fondation Singer-Polignac, Paris. Organized by the British Council.

CHAPTER 2

THE CHANGING MARKET-PLACE

WHAT ARE we witnessing when Ricardo Semler of Semco in Brazil refuses to be called 'boss', and prefers the term 'counsellor'; when Julian Richer of Richer Sounds refers to his employees as 'colleagues'; when UK retailer John Lewis calls its workforce 'partners'; and the manufacturers of Gore-Tex call their employees 'associates'? When an annual survey of Gore-Tex associates found that 50 per cent of them – 3,000 people – regard themselves in some way as leaders, is it trendy 'political correctness', or evidence of something more profound? I believe it is the latter. These organizations have discovered – some of them quite a long time ago – that there is competitive advantage in treating employees in such a way that their potential to make a unique contribution to the organization is acknowledged.

A central argument of this book is that organizations need to respond to a revolution in the market-places in which they operate. The rise in importance of individual thought and action is both an inevitable consequence of, and a strategic response to, the most profound changes that are affecting the way we live and work. Those who work in organizations therefore face a fundamental challenge – to re-create those organizations as places in which individuals can really contribute. A half-contributing workforce will no longer be acceptable in an age when organizations will need fewer people with greater responsibilities.

There is a sense among thinking managers and corporate leaders of the enormity of the change facing organizations. Many also acknowledge that responses to date have not really dealt with the totality of the modifications that need to be made as a result. Many others are reluctant to take on board the issues, which seem too abstract and theoretical for the pragmatic world of organizational life (sometimes referred to as the 'real world'). Yet the changes affecting us now will surely alter everything; the managers and organizations which succeed will be those that find the time to look beyond the inwardly focused world of management, and realize that each organization is a servant of the market. In addition, the market is profoundly changing the relationship between individual and organization.

The rise of the individual is a response to an increasingly competitive market-place. It is driven by it at two levels. First, it is a result of the new operating conditions in the markets themselves – including the fact that the individuals employed by organizations, in some cases, will be an increasingly powerful force; and, second, it is driven by the changes that organizations will have to make to their internal structures and processes if they are to deal successfully with these conditions.

THE POWER OF COMPETITION

Market volatility – the need to keep changing by adapting and innovating, and to respond to forces outside the direct control of an organization – can be characterized by a general increase in the intensity of the competition experienced by most organizations. New competitors arriving on the scene, new technologies, changes in legislation, changes in the status of existing competitors, and so on, can all lead to an increase in competition.

A friend and colleague, David Brech, has developed a 'strategy quiz'[1] which is used with top teams and strategy groups all over the world. It allows organizations to measure their managers' perception of the market volatility they face, in terms of how they are expected to respond across a number of different variables. These variables include defending price, improving operating costs and margins, bringing new products to market, manage the risk of take-overs, and so on. The quiz also measures the managers' perception of the organization's ability to respond to demands. The results are interesting.

World-wide, private and public organizations report anticipated steep increases in market volatility; in some industries, such as pharmaceuticals, the predicted increase is as much as 36 per cent. Organizations differ considerably in the supply-side shortfall they perceive – in other words, their ability to meet demands – with some recognizing considerable shortfalls. This work brings home in a very straightforward way where an organization needs to start building its strategic response. There will be several components to this response, however, it will almost always require an organization to establish new, more innovative, more responsive ways of working, as well as a new relationship with the individuals it employs.

The volatility is driven by a whole range of different factors, which can be summarized in terms of a handful of major geopolitical and technological developments, to which virtually all organizations have had to respond:

- technological change – the 'communications revolution';
- globalization;
- privatization;
- demographic changes.

TECHNOLOGICAL CHANGE – THE 'COMMUNICATIONS REVOLUTION'

The speed of change is driven by the speed of technology. Virtually every one of the changes facing organizations can find its origins in the technological revolution. For example, information technology has made financial institutions part of a global network, enabling the rapid movement of capital; no organization, or government, can ultimately protect itself from the effects of this. IT has globalized the local market-place and globalized the process of production.

The speed and volume of information exchange has done more than simply connect the financial systems of the world, or facilitate low-cost typesetting. To a large extent, it has also linked the social, cultural and political systems of the world. A major connecting force, the software, is capable of carrying information in the form of 'media content, music, computer games',[2] as well as computer programming software, quickly and cheaply to every part of the world. The result is that the world, most obviously through the Internet, is interlocked. There is no longer any reason why a political, social, economic or environmental change in one part of the world cannot have an almost immediate impact on an organization in another.

Almost as soon as an event happens, news of that event travels around the world. Financial markets can react immediately. Organizations cannot. Often, they have hardly begun to react to one set of circumstances before a development somewhere else starts to demand a response. The result is a feeling of loss of control, and a determination to become more responsive.

These changes have affected organizations at every level. They have changed the people, the processes, the management systems, the strategy, and the environment in which they operate.

The people have changed because a different set of skills is needed. IT has, at the same time, both de-skilled and up-skilled the demands of work. There is a bi-polarized workforce, with an insecure and low-skilled group on the one hand, and a highly skilled, increasingly qualified group on the other. The expectations of the second group go far beyond the exchange of security for compliance that characterized their relationship with work in the past. These are the 'knowledge workers', the owners and processors of the highly portable commodity of information.

The location of people's work has also changed. Digital communication means that most back-office and some customer-service functions can be moved to wherever they can be carried out most cost-effectively. It also gives some employees the opportunity to choose where they work.

The management systems have changed because of the speed and volume of information now available. In the past, one of the major tasks of middle management was to ferry information up and down the organization. That aspect of the role is not obsolete, but it is much less important. Middle managers now have to be information managers, selecting which information is important, and acting on their own initiative to find trends across the organization that may be relevant to the activities in which they are involved.

Strategy has changed because organizations have to build the advance of technology into their assumptions. In many sectors – communications, for example – this involves constructing a scenario based on something that may not have been invented yet. The result is that strategy becomes much more contingent, and organizations have to build greater flexibility into themselves as a result.

The IT revolution has therefore radically altered the operating conditions for most organizations – exposing them to changes on a global basis (see also below) which can occur at often bewildering speed. So how will organizations begin to cope?

The solution lies in the problem. Better information and communications also enable organizations to be more responsive. In a way, therefore, technological development has created the potential for a virtuous circle. Renaissance Organizations exploit this potential by using communications technology to create integrative information flows that allow motivated people to take more autonomous and innovative action.

THE GLOBAL MARKET

The years since the Second World War have seen the gradual opening up of the global market-place. Each time a barrier has come down, an opportunity and a threat are created – an opportunity to develop a new market, and a threat of new competition. Initially, this did not involve a major organizational challenge. The response might have involved setting up overseas sales and marketing offices, and perhaps sourcing production in low-wage economies. As international trade continues to grow, it becomes clear that many organizations will have to change more fundamentally if they are going to be successful in the global marketplace.

Specifically, an organization has to be able to operate equally effectively anywhere in the world, or it runs the risk of losing out to a company that can. This lays down an almost contradictory challenge – the consistency/inconsistency dilemma (see Chapter 1). It means that an organization has to be big enough to be able to deliver goods and services to global markets on the basis of the maximum possible economies of scale. At the same time, it has to be focused enough to compete with the local market leaders in every market in which it operates. Many organizations have responded by increasing their scale (through mergers and acquisitions, in particular), and by passing greater responsibility to local managers, to ensure local sensitivity. Moreover, in even medium-sized businesses, the advantages of scale will not only result from cost savings, but from the ability to exploit innovative potential from the ideas that arise in different parts of the business.

CONNECTIONS: BORN GLOBAL

It would be wrong to assume that global operations are the preserve of very large organizations. Local markets can be within the reach of even medium-sized companies from other parts of the world. This is not a particularly new phenomenon. The powerhouse of the German economy, the medium-sized businesses known as the *Mittelstand*, has often produced companies with a leading global market position within particular market niches on the basis of turnovers of around $125 million. Prof. Hermann Simon has argued in *Hidden Champions* that they have been able to do this because they are more open to change, make decisions more rapidly, and are more flexible and innovative than their larger competitors. One example is Fischerwerke, a fastenings company, which holds 5,500 patents, or 234 per employee, compared with the 10 patents per 100 employees held by Siemens, a reasonably innovative global organization.

The capacity for small to medium-sized organizations both to compete and be competed with globally, will, according to Katherine Campbell,[3] increase. The possibilities of the Internet, and of using IT to create 'virtual businesses', means that small companies can operate globally. And they may even need to if they are to gain business from large customers who also operate throughout the world. Thus, the threat of globalization is also an opportunity for business. Campbell quotes Peter Spraque, former chairman of National Semiconductor and founder of Wave Systems, which develops metering systems for databases, who says:

You want to know how we go global? It would be much weirder if you asked how we were going to stay local. The Internet forces you to be global, you literally don't have a choice.

As well as creating opportunities, the globalization of the market-place has also created an intense competition for customers. Organizations' structures are increasingly focused upon finding ever more effective ways of meeting customers' needs. They have also had to find new ways of building competitive advantage.

Three important factors underpin the ability of an organization to compete: the price of labour, the price of capital and the level of human capital (that is to say, learning, knowledge and skills, and the innovation that can lead from the effective exploitation of these). In Europe and North America, organizations are becoming increasingly dependent on the last of these determinants. This is because the price of unskilled labour in developed economies will always be higher than it is in developing economies. Higher savings rates, together with state involvement in allocating capital at below cost, for example, in the Far East, have made it difficult for organizations in Western nations to compete on the price of capital. Instead, they have to compete on the basis of human capital.

Another way of putting this is to say that the only competitive advantage that the developed world has is its numbers of well-educated people. In every other respect, other countries have already proved that they can catch up rapidly. They are able to achieve the skills-based manufacturing training that allows them to gain a rapid presence as an economic power, and, even in the area of education, they can improve. However, creating the educational infrastructure to ensure an adequate supply of knowledge workers seems to take longer than creating a body of skilled manufacturing workers.

As organizations have become more adept at seeking out competitive advantage, they have also found themselves more dependent on the intellectual skills of their employees. This has led to a power shift, creating a class of people who have no formal managerial power, and yet are enormously important to the organization.

Privatization

The trend towards privatization has spread from Britain to the rest of Europe because of rising public expenditure, concern about efficiency in publicly owned industries, and a universal reluctance to pay more tax. Outside Europe, there is less of a tradition of the welfare state, but there has been a step back from regulation in the US, and, in the Far East, the exposure of cronyism is likely to have the effect of breaking links between the government and business.

Privatization obviously has the greatest effect on the industries that are directly involved. In some cases, such as the British coal industry, it can be a euphemism for extinction. In other cases, such as the UK bus industry, it can bring about a revitalization. Few organizations have not felt the impact in some way of the experience of privatization or deregulation.

Turning on its head a sector that is responsible for a large proportion of GDP and, directly or indirectly, employs a significant part of the workforce naturally has some effect on the rest of the economy. The most interesting effect is the way in which it changes employees' expectations of employers and employment, right across the economy. The public sector used to be able to offer its employees jobs for life, with steady salary increments and a pension at the end of it. In doing so, it set the norms for employment. The larger private-sector organizations often offered similar terms and conditions. Employees had a sense of the employer's responsibility that went beyond just paying a salary for a job done.

Of course, privatization alone was not responsible for the end of this expectation of paternalism. The experience of high unemployment and the retreat from demand management in the economy, as well as a number of other social factors, helped introduce a market-based attitude towards employers and employment. This attitude is deeply individualist. It says, 'I only work here as long as you can offer me a better future than any other employer can.' The loyalty to the employer that went with a guarantee of employment for life has gone.

To make matters worse for employers, it is the skilled staff – the ones with all the human capital, who represent the ability to create competitive advantage – who are most mobile. Not only do employers have to depend on them more, but they are also more likely to lose them. The senior managers who repeat the old saw 'our people are our greatest asset' forget that those people can turn into their greatest liability when they decide to walk to the opposition. The result of this is that there will be a group of individuals within organizations – not necessarily managers – who have potentially less loyalty and more power.

The management challenge tackled in this book will be:

- to keep key staff as long as possible and not assume their loyalty; and
- to maximize their value while they are with the manager's company.

Both challenges will require an organizational response that takes account of employees' individuality and needs, and engages them in far more than a compliance-for-cash relationship.

DEMOGRAPHICS

The rise of the individual will also be driven in the future by the simple fact that there will – in developed economies – be fewer people, and that not all of those will be willing or able to work in traditional ways. Demographic changes are always slow, but their inevitability lends them urgency. Several strands have been highlighted, the most important of which are:

- more women are returning to work after having children;
- birth rates in developed countries are slowing down, while people are living longer;
- populations are expanding fastest in developing countries.

The fact that more women are returning to work puts employers under pressure to offer greater flexibility in their terms of employment. Although there is no law to force organizations to offer this flexibility, if they want to continue to benefit from the time, information and other resources they have invested in these people, it will become necessary.

This flexibility is not always straightforward. In most organizations, power and responsibility go with presence. It is a challenge for organizations to integrate flexible working patterns without demotivating staff by removing responsibility. Organizations need to take a different view of their employees. Working to the traditional nine to five day, employers have expected employees to cut out their home life when they get to work. Parents (and especially mothers) cannot do this so easily, and employers who want to get the most out of them need to recognize this fact. Seeing the whole person, rather than just the worker, is the key to motivation in the Renaissance Organization.

Slowing birth rates and the ageing population create a totally different challenge for the organization. As the proportion of the population who are active in the economy decreases, the active have to become more productive, to make up for the rising number of unproductive people. This is not just because of the increased burden of state benefits on the economy. Private pensions are dependent on the returns of investment in the stock exchange and annuity rates. These are both related to growth in the economy. In Japan, for example, where economic growth has been flat for most of the 1990s, interest rates have fallen as low as 0.5 per cent and annuity yields are very small: £100,000 might buy a pension of no more than £1,000 per year. Unless a generation of pensioners is to be impoverished, the economy needs to continue to grow.

The solution lies in developing the human capital – the skills, knowledge and abilities of the people – within the economy. As Peter Drucker[4] has explained, with falling populations, economic growth cannot come from more people in work (supply side) or more local consumption (demand side). It has to come from greater investment in human capital.

One of the implications of becoming a more knowledge-based economy is that, by its very nature, it will be more volatile. Knowledge is always reinventing itself. It soon becomes obsolete, and new knowledge needs to be generated. The volatility of the computer industry illustrates the possible effect of a switch to a knowledge-based economy. Through its own search to renew itself, knowledge can cause sudden changes in what is seen as important, as a new discovery, or even fashion, emphasizes new areas of expertise.

The nature of this work will require a contribution that is built upon much more than technical skills and compliance. Jobs will have to be built from the whole contribution an individual can make and, in return, organizations will have to find ways of meeting individual employees' needs much more specifically than they have done in the past.

The implications of an ageing population in developed countries will also be seen, both in changes in customer demands in all aspects of products and services, and in the way that organizations manage their workforce. The number of people over 35 in the workforce in the UK is expected to increase by 1.8 million between 1995 and 2001, while the number aged under 35 is set to decrease by 0.9 million. It may no longer be so easy to renew a workforce to meet the need to change by selecting younger people and disregarding those who are felt to be set in their ways. Companies that try it will find it expensive, because demand for younger workers will exceed supply. Instead, organizations will have to find ways of remotivating and enthusing an older generation, which may, through experience, have found reasons to be cynical and demotivated. Development, more than selection, will be the key tool in building a competitive workforce. As work is likely to be knowledge-based and, therefore, continually changing, then development will also have to be continuous – this fact is increasingly recognized at corporate and government levels.

UNPREDICTABILITY

Organizations are not just facing rapid and complex change; they are also facing increasing uncertainty. Change feeds upon itself. The more responsive organizations make themselves in order to cope with changing competitive demands, the more what used to be regarded as responsive is seen as barely adequate. The result is that the frontier of what is acceptable is continually moving forwards. When this is fuelled by parallel advances in IT, change can be very rapid indeed and, because of the inter-connectedness of the market-place, it can also be unpredictable.

In the past, management was about planning, control and forecasting, and individuals fulfilled their part within the master plan. However, the unpredictability is bound to change all this. Organizations will have to work out how they operate in a market-place that may be better understood as being structured as a complex, interlocked system. The behaviour of complex systems is a new area and a controversial field of research across science. Its implications for the operation of markets and organizations could be profound. (One very interesting feature of complex systems is their capacity for self-organization. They produce recognizable patterns from the interplay of their constituent parts. The implications for this in the way that local groups respond to the complexity of a distant senior management and a local complex reality are intriguing!)

New insights are emerging from those studying the economic and business world from the point of view of complexity theory. These theories suggest that the ability of organizations and managers to work in the planned, controlled way suggested by classical management theorists is strictly limited. Complexity lives near the edge of chaos, and chaos theory says that wildly unpredictable patterns and events can be determined by a few simple dynamic rules. Complex systems, such as organizations and the environments in which they exist, operate just on the right side of chaos. There is a balance point at which the patterns of behaviour never quite seem to fit together perfectly, but they never collapse into disarray either. A feature of such systems is that they can seem to change quite spontaneously, and that small differences within parts of them can alter completely the nature of the whole system.

Such insights run counter to the traditional economic view of market behaviour. In that view, there is a tendency towards an equilibrium in which supply is balanced by demand, and in which the laws of diminishing returns regulate the ability of an organization to dominate the market. This ordered view of the world of neo-classical economists shows a movement towards a situation of stability and order. In such a situation, good businesses will usually thrive, because they are efficient and better than their competitors.

According to the purist and rational view of economic theory, the free market will winnow out the best and most efficient technologies, leaving lesser technologies to fall by the wayside.

However, according to the economist and complexity theorist Brian Arthur, in Mitchell Waldrop's[5] account of the development of complexity theory so far, these ideas do not reflect the real world in which businesses operate and people work. Rather than see a movement towards equilibrium, Arthur sees markets as dynamic and evolving, capable of spontaneous change, constantly unfolding, and full of patterns, possibilities and surprises. He notes that, rather than a law of decreasing returns, there is plenty of evidence of a phenomenon he calls 'increasing returns'. Increasing returns occur when the conditions are such that a small difference will have an enormous effect on the whole system, as the effect amplifies the difference, which in turn amplifies the effect. In other words, a reinforcing loop occurs. A classic example of this, he argues, is the VHS vs Beta battle of the video systems in the mid-1970s. Many experts suggested that Beta was technically the better system, yet in the end VHS came to dominate the market totally.

Arthur has shown mathematically, and through numerous examples, how seemingly random events can have an enormous impact on the system. After a market gets 'locked in' to a particular approach, sometimes in spite of varying degrees of technical excellence, the result is that a pattern can rapidly grow to dominate the market for a while, either organizationally, or in terms of dominant technology (as with Microsoft).

The consequence of this is that it is very difficult to identify the rules by which the market-place is going to behave. As a result, organizations in certain industries will have to learn to adapt to these 'surprises' and irrational lock-ins.

CONNECTIONS: 'THE CASINO OF INCREASING RETURNS'

Not all industries are in parts of the economic system that create conditions for 'increasing returns'. Bulk processing industries are not usually troubled by this sort of volatility; for them, optimization is usually the most important strategy. High-tech industries are very different. Brian Arthur[6] likens this to playing a gambling game in a casino, where you do not know who the players are, you are not sure of the rules and you cannot calculate the odds. On top of that, you are obliged to bet heavily:

You cannot optimize in the casino of increasing returns games. You can be smart. You can be cunning. You can position. You can observe. But, when the games themselves are not even fully defined, you cannot optimize. What you can do is adapt. Adaptation, in the pro-active sense, means watching out for the next wave that is coming, figuring out what shape it will take, and positioning the company to take advantage of it.

Positioning, adaptivity, flexibility and responsiveness are all key themes of Renaissance Management.

It seems that in all complex systems there is a 'pocket of predictability'. For a system like the weather, it is probably 5–10 days. This limit to the predictability of the weather occurs despite the fact there are a finite number of variables within the weather system, and that the relationships between them are well mapped out. What about an economic system or a business system? It could be argued that organizations, too, operate within a pocket of predictability. According to Brian Cunningham, formerly a senior executive with IBM (now visiting professor at Ulster Business School), and a truly innovative manager,

the concept applies to any particular market. Competitive markets only behave predictably within close-in horizons. Beyond these horizons lie chaos and unpredictability. Likewise business processes within any one company work up to a certain level beyond which they stall... chaos will reign for a while and a new system will be installed.[7]

Paul Thorne has put it this way:

> *Above all else, people who run companies seek control. To reach control they have to find means of predicting outcome. If the world says to them, such means are no longer available, then they are left with little option but to innovate ways of maintaining control without predictability.*[8]

The impact of complexity theory on our understanding of markets and organizations is at an early stage, but it has already suggested the very limited power we have to predict and manipulate the market. On the other hand, many of these effects of complex systems can be shown to arise from the operation of relatively few different variables. Therefore, the more we can understand those variables, the more we might extend the pocket of predictability, and learn to respond more effectively to both complex and chaotic events in our market-places.

Long chains of management and fixed procedures defining what someone is going to do, and how, would seem to be an inadequate response to these conditions. Thinking, empowered, connected individuals may well be the answer.

Market alignment

How an organization has to respond to these forces also provides impetus for a greater focus on the contribution of individuals. The next chapters deal specifically with the ways in which an organization can respond in an energetic way to market conditions. It is worth reviewing those conditions here, in terms of their impact on the rise of the individual.

How will organizations cope with conditions of change and unpredictability? One of the ways suggested by Brian Arthur is to be fantastically well aligned to the chances and opportunities of the market-place. One route to alignment is to ensure high levels of responsiveness and adaptability. This includes being more responsive to customer needs, to unexpected opportunities and to threats from new technologies and competitors, to local needs, as well as to synergies that exist between different parts of the organization (particularly for organizations comprised of several different business units). Organizations need to make sure everyone is focused on what is happening, in a position to make local responses if necessary, and willing and able to communicate the reality of the market-place as they find it to their organization as a whole.

To become more responsive, organizations need to change their internal operation. First, responsibility has to be decentralized, so that decisions about how to react to changes in the market can be made and executed as close to the front line as possible. This cuts out the need for information to find its way up to the top of the organization, and orders to find their way back to the bottom before anything can be done. This arrangement makes success more dependent on people further down the organization. Previously, many of these people tended to be defined on a functional basis, but, if the organization is to be responsive, they have to be able to act and think across functions.

As a result of this, people have to become more adaptable. They have to be able to work in different ways, and intelligently, so that they change the way they work as circumstances change.

Organizations will become more dependent on the skills and outlook of their members, and will only be able to change in ways that their people can change. This may sound very restrictive, but the alternative – changing the people as circumstances change – is not only expensive, but is also unlikely to work. If a job were advertised every time it changed, many jobs would be permanent vacancies, because the recruitment process would not be able to keep up with the rate of change.

Instead, organizations have to get the best out of their people. This means ensuring that their interests are compatible with the interests of their members. They cannot rely on salaries (there is never enough money to buy the best of everyone), or fear (which undermines any willingness to take the initiative). Instead, they have to understand the more complex motivations that make people commit to an organization.

Differentiation through Innovation and Diversity

Many organizations have focused on responsiveness and adaptability as ways of dealing with volatility. Others have emphasized a second strategy – strategic positioning – reducing the impact of competition by being different to, as well as better than, their competitors. This market alignment is achieved by creatively configuring an organization's offer so that it meets a customer's needs in a way that is difficult to replicate. If being responsive requires innovative behaviour, being different needs it even more.

There is something very individualistic about this. Innovation is based upon individual contribution, not compliance with the status quo and convention. The basis for innovation is, at its most elemental level, the action or thought of an individual. The conditions in which innovation can most easily be secured are a by-product of developing responsiveness – differentiation and diversity.

The argument for differentiation holds true at both organizational and individual level. Organizations seem to gain benefit from maintaining as many options, ways of doing things, and characteristics as possible, and then finding the means effectively to mobilize them. Nohria and Ghoshal,[9] in a study of multi-national corporations, found that 'diversity through internal differentiation is essential to optimal firm performance', and that

> *overall subsidiary performance is correlated with a high degree of internal differentiation, in the same way that differentiation is required for enhancing innovation.*

The ultimate inspiration for differentiation and, therefore, the wellspring of innovation and competitive advantage, is the thought, will and action of individuals. Particularly important is their ability to draw on the complex variety of their experience, and associated ideas and insights, to create novel solutions and opportunities.

Of course, there is a limit to the differentiation and diversity of ideas and approaches with which an organization can cope. However, with creativity and imagination, and trust, most organizations could cope with much more diversity than they do at present. Integration as a counterbalancing force does not have to be achieved by the over-constraining, over-controlling, directive means employed by many organizations to date. (Strategies for integration that encourage diversity are tackled in Chapter 6.)

THE ENERGY FOR MANAGING PARADOX

The overall impact of change leading to the rise of the individual in organizations can be summarized as follows. Organizations need to:

1. establish a step change in levels of responsiveness and innovation by radical developments in local decision-making and individual action;
2. find ways of integrating this local and individual action with the needs of the business, without over-restricting and limiting the contribution they can make;
3. build, where possible, clear differentiation from competitors and encourage diversity;
4. put greater emphasis on human capital, based on the needs and whole potential of each individual;
5. respond to the fact that key staff are becoming more mobile between organizations;
6. organize themselves more flexibly, both in terms of employment arrangements but also in the roles people undertake – with an increasing amount of self-definition of contribution.

The first three points identify, through innovation and responsiveness, the market alignment constituent of the virtuous energy cycle established in Chapter 1, while the last three represent the individual focus.

For most organizations, responding to these forces will require revolutionary measures. Building and managing organizations based on individuals, not roles, challenges managers to think in totally new ways about communication, performance management, development and training, and target-setting. Furthermore, much of what is required of individuals is essentially paradoxical. The twin forces of integration and differentiation lead to inconsistency in individual action, and the following are required: conformity and challenge, a focus on goals and a spirit of experimentation, team play and individual action, employees who want to learn and grow, and to take control of their work and development and also, at times, sublimate their own needs for the greater good. A high-performing workforce in volatile conditions needs not only to be encouraged to show a broader range of behaviours and greater commitment, but diversity at individual, team and organizational level also need to be welcomed and encouraged. As we shall see in Chapter 5, in the work of Michael Apter, inconsistency and paradox are the hallmark of human nature; traditional organizational perspectives have denied this, and ignored the potential contribution.

The conditions of change will have a different impact on different organizations, and on how they will need to respond. For some large organizations, the necessary changes will be dramatic. Others – especially those operating in mature markets, which are sheltered from international competition – may find things changing more insidiously. For organizations at the cutting edge of technology, this way of operating may already be a fact of life.

For all organizations, operating in the way described will require different kinds of energy:

- organizational energy, to realize the latent potential and diversity of the workforce;
- increased energy from individuals, which will be reflected in new ways of working;
- energy to convince individuals that it is worth changing and contributing;

- energy to provide the decision-making and communication processes that will mobilize the individual's contribution;
- energy to integrate this diversity without constricting it;
- energy to accommodate the mistakes that will be made; and
- energy to innovate.

Unfortunately, energy is a commodity that seems to be in short supply in many organizations.

Where will this energy be found, and how will it be financed? The benefits should be a vastly increased contribution from the workforce, but, in lean times, who can afford to invest? The strategy must be to create higher levels of energy flow – more energy going in and coming out, in a virtuous innovation cycle – in which organizational competitive advantage creates energy. This energy is used to realize individual energy for responsiveness and innovation, which leads to further competitive advantage. Is it worth the investment? Organizations have no choice.

The energy cycle is the key feature of Renaissance Organization. It is the opposite of costs strategies (which are inevitably low-energy), in which training budgets are cut, environmental improvements are curtailed, and communication technology is not properly financed, and are likely to be inadequate to link the diversity and creativity of the business.

To begin to make sense of the management challenge, it will be useful to spend some time in the next chapter thinking more about what energy is, and how it can be gained at an organizational level.

REFERENCES

1. Further details can be obtained from: Agenda for Change, PO Box 2000, Stroud, Gloucestershire, UK.
2. Technology foresight report no 14 (1995) *Leisure and learning,* HMSO, London.

3. Campbell, K (1997) The global company: the minnows' fight against the sharks, the *Financial Times*, 24 October.
4. Drucker, P *et al* (Sept/Oct 1997) Looking ahead: implications of the present, *Harvard Business Review.*
5. Waldrop, M M (1993) *Complexity: The emerging science at the edge of order and chaos*, Touchstone Books, London.
6. Arthur, W B (1996) Increasing returns and the new world of business, *Harvard Business Review.*
7. Cunningham, B (1993) private paper, 'Lessons from complexity'.
8. Thorne, P (1989) *The New General Manager*, Henley Management Series, McGraw-Hill, Maidenhead.
9. Nohria, N and Ghoshal, S (1997) *The Differentiated Network*, Jossey Bass, California.

CHAPTER 3

CREATING A HIGH-ENERGY ORGANIZATION

THE ENERGY BALANCE

'Something has changed,' said Tom. 'Trading conditions are just as difficult, and some of our technologies are just as obsolete, and I guess we could still smarten up some of the ways we do things, but now we feel we can cope. Everyone's contributing and supporting each other, there's loads of ideas around and a feeling you can go ahead and get the job done without it all getting bogged down in politics and management. Even customers have noticed the difference and are asking for more!'

Tom is referring to a high-energy environment. Renaissance Organizations actively seek to build such an environment, in which individuals can maximally contribute the breadth and depth of their potential. An alignment of energy flows between market and organization, and between organization and individual, is created.

To achieve this, it is essential to understand more about what energy means in terms of organizations. How can the concept be characterized and operationalized, so that organizations may be structured in such a way as to build high-energy flows? Once this concept is understood, organizations can be designed for high energy, and can capture the responsiveness and innovation driven by individual contribution. A virtuous cycle can be created.

Energy, a means to an end as well as an end in itself, gives organizations the capacity to change. They need it so that they can be better, and they are better as a result of having it.

To find out how organizations can be energized, it is necessary to take them apart and look at how energy works within them (see Fig. 3.1 for a simplified view of the idea that organizations exist to let four basic stakeholders exchange energy in order to gain benefit individually). Customers exchange money for goods or services that they regard as valuable, shareholders invest funds, expecting them to be returned with added value, suppliers sell raw materials, and employees trade their effort in return for wages. So far, so simple.

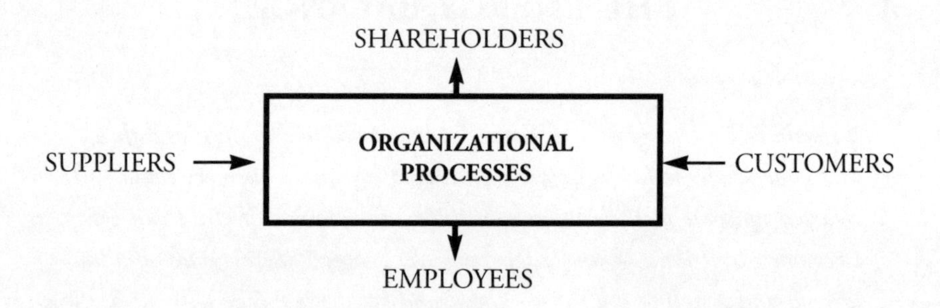

Fig. 3.1 The four basic stakeholders

However, it is not so simple. There are actually many more transactions in this system than the financial ones, and it is not possible to establish objectively what is of value. For example, a supplier will deal with an organization for more than one reason; it may want to be seen to be doing so, and, as well as raw materials for money, reputation is being exchanged. In addition, a supplier may give preferential rates because a customer is seen as secure. Customers' buying decisions are based on more than technical specification; for example, the way the customer has been dealt with will be part of the way both sides view the value of the transaction. Nowadays many organizations understand customer value in terms of an ongoing relationship rather than the short-term transaction. Energy is required to create such a relationship, but is also stored in it, and it therefore has ongoing value. (An example of the complexity of the energy exchanges in consumer transactions is reflected in the willingness of customers of branded goods to turn themselves into advertising hoardings by wearing the name of the supplier.)

The final and very important example of non-financial aspects of energy transactions are those between the organization and the people who work for it. Employees want more from their work than just a salary, and the value they create will be directly related to a total energy equation – what they are asked to put in, balanced against what they expect to get out.

Some argue that, in the end, the value of all these transactions will be judged in the purely financial terms of long-term shareholder value. Ongoing shareholder value is a useful way of looking beyond the short-term horizon of the profit and loss account and the balance sheet, but any assessment of an organization will be more relevant if the overall energy equation of the organization is taken into account. Such an assessment should include a broad range of human factors, including customer relationships and motivational climate (see Chapter 5).

A Renaissance approach emphasizes the fact that the relationship of an organization to its market-place needs to be considered not only in financial terms, but also in human terms, looking at attitudes, feelings, perceptions, and so on. These factors characterize the energy available to an organization as much as, if not more than the assets on the balance sheet. When an organization undertakes an employee or customer survey, it is measuring the energy it has available for change. The human factors that emerge will suggest whether or not an organization has the energy to adapt to change and make itself great.

An understanding and assessment of the topography of human

energy within an organization leads to a deeper understanding, not just of the relationship of stakeholders to the organization, but also of the relationship between stakeholders – how employee energy has an impact upon the customer energy transaction.

A Renaissance Organization will establish effective ways of monitoring human energy with all stakeholders. It will also work to create positive energy flows at three levels: at the individual level, at the organizational systems level, and at the market positioning level. By managing energy effectively at all three levels, an organization builds an environment in which there is energy for change. This chapter, analysing at the organizational and market level, deals with the non-employee stakeholders in the energy system. At the individual level, Renaissance Management will be clear about how it wants individuals to contribute energy in the future – what form this energy should take, and also the basis upon which individuals might feel able to contribute (see Chapters 4 and 5).

ENERGY AND ORGANIZATIONAL SYSTEMS

As well as ensuring that they have access to all the different kinds of energy a person and a market can offer, the organization has to ensure that it does not waste this energy in inefficient organizational systems. The energy that people put into organizations is absorbed in a number of ways. Some of it is used for actually doing things for the customer, such as adding value to a product or service, but very little of it is directly productive in this way! Much of it is spent communicating with other people within the organization, co-ordinating activities, planning, motivating, managing, being managed. There are also a number of social activities, such as chatting and drinking coffee, which are not necessarily condoned by the organization, but probably contribute in some way to its well-being.

Change probably absorbs the most energy. Energy is needed to implement new systems, structures and processes, for people to learn new behaviours and skills, for managers to develop new ways of managing, and for the rebuilding of relationships between people within the organization. Change may also require capital investment, but energy is what it feeds on most, and it can be a bottomless pit if the organization does not respond to it.

Each time we do something, some of our energy is converted into what we have done. Sometimes, we get back energy from doing it. If we find it rewarding, for example, or if we find it suits our own objectives, and what we want to get out of the organization, the activity may energize us.

It is easy to see why some start-up operations have the energy advantage. They are small enough to avoid dissipating their energy in an elaborate corporate structure. They are also better at engaging the whole personality of their members. This can create a virtuous circle, in which members of the organization use their creativity, their learning ability, and their team dynamic to respond successfully to change. They will often find themselves energized by this success, and will commit still more of their potential to the organization. This gives start-ups tremendous energy. They have a greater capacity for change, are more adept at seizing opportunities, and are proportionally more ambitious than established organizations.

Most organizations lose this energy as they become established. In fact, an energetic established organization is almost a contradiction in terms. However, that is what an organization has to be if it is to continue to prosper.

Large organizations find it more difficult to be energetic. Size can cause problems in conserving energy, and large organizations also find it more difficult to tap into the whole personality of their employees. The problems are mainly rooted in their organizational systems. They need to find ways of re-creating themselves that capture the high-energy environment of a small business.

Jack Welch of General Electric has characterized it this way:

We set out to shape a global enterprise that preserved the big-company advantages while eliminating the classic big-company drawbacks. What we wanted

> *to build was a hybrid, an enterprise with the reach and resources of a big company, but the thirst to learn, the compulsion to share and the bias for action – the soul – of a small company.*[1]

A Renaissance Organization will constantly strive to achieve this scale without mass, driven by individual action and enthusiasm, but aiming to remain an integrated, cohesive entity.

ENERGY AND MARKET POSITIONS

The Renaissance Organization has one advantage over the newly born one – it can exploit the innate energy of its market position.

Organizations gain energy from their market-place. Most obviously, they gain energy in the form of money by selling goods and services for a profit. This creates the energy that sustains the organization. There are also other, more subtle ways in which organizations can gain energy from the market-place – through developing awareness of their brand, building goodwill among their customers and their suppliers, and getting to know the market-place.

Organizations can also lose energy to the market-place. They can lose it to competitors, or by failing to keep up with change in the market-place. They can lose it to suppliers, if their suppliers are in a strong position to dictate terms. They can also lose it to suppliers if those suppliers are unreliable.

The main way an organization can ensure that it gains energy from its market-place is to establish a strong market position, in which it gets the best possible results for the least possible effort. With its virtually ubiquitous Windows operating system, Microsoft has created a virtually unassailable position in its particular market. To use a sporting analogy, it has created a situation in which it not only produces the means to play the game, but also controls the rules of the game. An article in *Fortune*[2] magazine highlighted a growing realization in the world of software that 'everyone in the software game today needs a Microsoft strategy' and that every small company '[has] to find a way to work with [them], if [it] want[s] to survive and thrive'.

The companies in the weakest market position are those that are among a number of different players competing with similar offers. Customers expect more and more features as standard, and ever-improving performance for the same price. 3M executives may have found themselves in this situation when they decided to close down one of the company's businesses, in which it was a world leader.

3M is admired by its peers and very attractive to potential employees. The company environment is challenging, and demands high levels of innovation – 10 per cent of annual sales are targeted as coming from sales that did not exist a year ago, and 30 per cent of revenues should come from products that are less than four years old. Overall, 3M seeks a return of 27 per cent on capital employed.[3]

In July 1996, 3M closed down a part of the business in which it had led the world. Executives were convinced that this market sector had become one in which there was no chance to make the sort of returns they were seeking.

The organization in the strongest market position is the one that offers a unique must-have – the clear market leader in a market for one. Being the clear market leader in a more competitive market is often a good second best, but it can turn out to be a low-energy position, because so much effort is required in terms of discounts, marketing or continuous product enhancements.

A powerful strategy is to carve out a protected niche. To do this, organizations have to try to be different. The more different an organization is considered to be, the less it will be in competition with other organizations. Energy can be taken from the market-place for less effort. But being different is not enough; an organization has to be absolutely market-focused on exactly how it is different.

STRATEGIC POSITIONING VS OPERATIONAL EFFICIENCY

An energy-based analysis of how organizations work indicates that a strong market position is as important as, if not more important than operational effectiveness in determining that organization's success.

Michael Porter[4] notes two main reasons why operating effectiveness – doing things better – is a necessary condition for competitive advantage, but is still not enough:

- the rapid diffusion of best practice means that improvement in performances is absolute across industry, and therefore gives no relative advantage to anyone;
- further, the more benchmarking organizations undertake, the more they begin to look alike, particularly if they start to outsource processes to the same third parties.

An organization requires a strategy about being different. In Porter's terms, that is almost saying the same thing twice; he would claim that strategy *is* being different. This is not to belittle the importance of being efficient, or of doing things as well as or better than the opposition. In fact, maximizing the efficiency with which processes are undertaken is an essential feature of Renaissance Organizations, but on its own it is unlikely to give an organization a long-term advantage.

Operational effectiveness has been characterized by a whole range of initiatives, including TQM, re-engineering and benchmarking. Such initiatives gave Japanese organizations their massive competitive advantage, enabling them to come up with products with added value at a cost for which Western organizations were unable to produce even a basic model. However, for the Japanese, it has been a game of diminishing returns.

In contrast, strategic positioning means carrying out activities that are different from those of rival organizations, or carrying out similar activities in different ways – meeting a customer's needs in a new way. Doing this includes both the creation of new ideas, and the re-bundling of old ideas in new ways, to give the customer added value.

The banking industry demonstrates these theories better than almost any other. Over the last few years, the market has seen dramatic innovations in positioning, which have changed the rather homogenous shape of the industry. These innovations have been not so much in terms of products, but in the way those products are accessed. In 1989, First Direct introduced a new and innovative form of banking in the UK, using advances in technology to operate a branchless network. It provides all its services through telephones and ATMs, which enables it to operate with a much lower cost base than banks that have to maintain a branch network.

Banks such as the MBNA Corporation have made other innovations in this area; it is really a single-offer business, offering only credit cards, and is backed less by the receipt of customer deposits and more by combining and selling loans as securities. Credit cards are now also available through non-bank sources such as General Motors and the Ford Motor Company.

On the other hand, bucking any trend away from one-stop banking is the new Virgin One account, a joint venture between Virgin Direct and the Royal Bank of Scotland, recently launched in the UK. This offer is a good example of strategic positioning. Previous innovation has moved away from what went before, to begin what might be thought of as the new orthodoxy – an increasing emphasis on banking focusing on single businesses – and Virgin is exploiting the space left behind. It is doing this by meeting the needs of those who 'have neither the time nor the inclination to shop around for financial products'.[5]

Connections: Innovation and Strategic Positioning

Kim and Mauborgne[6] carried out a study of over 30 organizations from around the world, looking for the roots of high growth. After extensive research, they found that none of the traditional assumptions about what made high-growth companies seemed to matter in a systematic way. High growth was found in organizations of all sizes, in both the public and private sector, in low and high tech, across national boundaries, and operating with high and low technologies. What seemed to matter most was how managers in low- and high-growth companies approached strategy:

The less successful companies took a conventional approach: their strategic thinking was dominated by the idea of staying ahead of the competition. In stark contrast, the high-growth companies paid little attention to matching or beating their rivals. Instead, they sought to make their rivals irrelevant through a strategic logic we call value innovation.

Among the companies examined by the authors, Virgin Atlantic was highlighted. The airline has one of the highest sales per employee in the industry, and its costs per passenger mile are among the lowest. Stating that the economics of value innovation create a positive and reinforcing cycle, Kim and Mauborgne claim that Virgin 'violated conventional wisdom by conceiving of its business in terms of customer solutions, even if that took the company well beyond an airline's traditional offerings'.

There are two routes to being different in the eyes of the consumer: innovation in branding, and innovation in design. The importance of each varies according to the market. Branding is the key to creating a difference in many consumer markets, but it has to be backed by innovation, both in terms of how the brand is developed, and in terms of how the product is developed. While there may be some design classics, most designs date, and organizations which aim to differentiate themselves on the basis of design (such as clothing or furniture manufacturers) have to innovate to ensure that their designs remain current. Innovation in all its guises is, therefore, the key to differentiation.

So innovation is not restricted to the specification of a product or service. In fact, in many instances, innovation aimed at improving the product would be a mistake; for example, Coca-Cola's decision to change the taste of its Coke was soundly rejected by the market. Innovation should extend to the delivery and the marketing of the product to the customer.

One example of this – H J Heinz's decision to pull out of consumer media advertising and to invest in direct marketing instead – was a profoundly innovative move. In the USA, Heinz has made supporting children's hospitals its primary marketing effort. For every Heinz baby food label posted back to the company, six cents is donated to a children's hospital. According to a company spokesman, 'Our share of the baby food market is up and this is the only programme we do. We don't do advertising, we don't do print, we don't do TV.'[7]

Positioning includes the total re-presentation of what an organization is offering to its customers – for example, the structure of the product or service offered, the way it is sold, the way it is packaged, and the way it is delivered and maintained. Put simply, organizations need to be innovative about what they *are* as well as about what they *do*:

> *Competitive advantage grows out of the entire system of activities. The fit among activities substantially reduces cost or increases differentiation. Beyond that, the competitive value of individual activities – or the associated skills, competencies, or resources – cannot be de-coupled from the system or the strategy.* [8]

If there is a competitive advantage residing in the whole system that makes up an organization, not just in one or two core activities, that organization gains enormously, because replication of what it offers and of its strategic position becomes very difficult. It achieves a very high-energy position in the market-place.

This response is summarized in Fig. 3.2. Organizations will probably find that different aspects of what they do fit in different parts of the quadrant. How would your organization place itself on here, both in overall terms and in respect of the different aspects of your business?

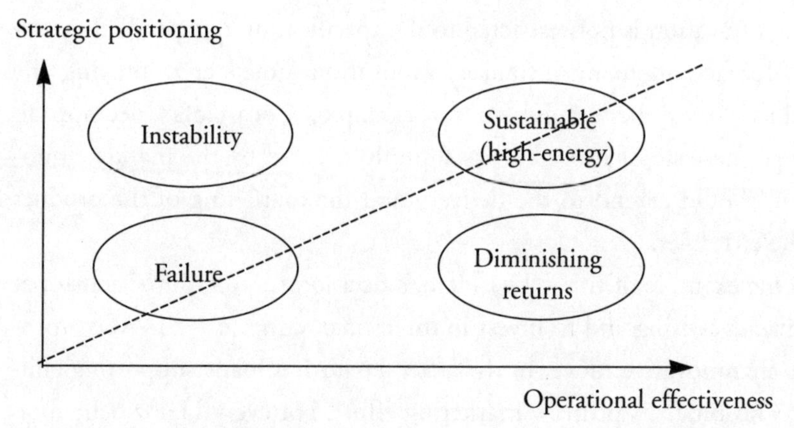

Fig. 3.2 Productive release of energy

RESPONSIVENESS – MEETING LOCAL NEEDS

Achieving a differentiated strategic position, in order to gain energy as effectively as possible from the market, does not come about through a 'one size fits all' approach. Strategic differentiation can also include local diversity – the need to respond to local conditions if an organization gains extra energy from doing so. For example, Unilever found that advanced laundry detergents, a major product line for the company, were not appropriate for markets such as India, where it is unusual for laundry to be done at home in a washing machine. The company has created a local adaptation – synthetic detergents in tablet form – and has captured a significant share of the market.

'Local' should not just refer to business-unit level; it can also mean seeing a particular customer as a market of one, and responding to that customer's needs. The responsiveness that characterizes a Renaissance Organization exists at all levels. The level of diversity – the extent to which an organization is prepared to suffer the 'inefficiencies' of inconsistency – is critical, and individuals need to be empowered to make decisions about it, and to have the understanding to do so. These might include decisions about one-off specials, different levels of service, and so on, and they need to be set within the context of long-term energy gain for the organization as a whole. This will require ways of measuring and communicating a common understanding of value (see Chapter 7).

The challenge for organizations will be to reconcile this local autonomy with the needs of the organization as a whole, so that innovations such as the Unilever example can be shared, if appropriate, with other parts of the business. This sharing of innovation – a key potential strength of larger companies – applies to products and services, and also to internal processes. If energy gain is not to be achieved expensively, organizations need to find ways to share innovation and keep consistent those things that give energy advantage from being consistent.

SUMMARY

Energy within organizations therefore needs to be seen in more than financial terms, if a longer-term view of the transactions involved is to be taken. A high-energy environment consists of meeting the energy needs of four key stakeholders. This chapter has focused principally on the relationship with customers, but many of the considerations would also have an impact upon shareholders and suppliers. There is much to be gained from considering how best they may contribute energy to an organization and what they might expect in return. (The fourth stakeholder group is discussed in Chapters 4 and 5.)

This chapter has also highlighted the way strategic positioning and local adaptability can help organizations maximize the way they gain energy from their relationship with their markets. This energy can be wasted through ineffective and over-elaborate internal processes and structures. Obtaining this energy requires high levels of innovation, and a workforce with new levels of decision-making authority and the ability to see their actions in terms of their impact on the organization as a whole.

Finally, a word of warning to those who might want to re-position a highly complex system such as an organization simply by copying another, to avoid the potential costs of true innovation. Strategic positioning depends on the innovative ability of an organization in all its intentions and activities. There is a limit to the amount that one organization can 'borrow' innovations from elsewhere. Replicating the complexity of systems that support innovation – or any other strategic activity – from one organization to another is very difficult. Because of the very nature of complex systems, it may sometimes be impossible.

CONNECTIONS: REPLICATING SUCCESS[9]

Jim Drake at Purdue University created a computer simulation of evolution, which consisted of 125 species of plants, herbivores and carnivores, with some simple rules that governed their evolution. Several interesting features emerged. First, after a period of initial chaos, a stable community of about 15 species appeared, which would successfully resist any attempt by Drake to introduce a new species, unless he introduced so many new species that chaos returned before settling down to a new stability within new 'pockets of predictability'. Each time the model was run from scratch, a different persistent community would appear and he never managed to replicate a world that previously existed. Further, if he tried to replicate the conditions of a stable community, he discovered that the previously stable world was not stable when entered as a starting set of conditions. He concluded that, unless the system went through precisely the same stages of development prior to the stable state, it would never reach the same stable state.

PROVOCATIONS

Checklist – do you have a high-energy environment for transformation?

To what extent does your product or service give potential customers advantages that they cannot get elsewhere?

Not at all			Completely	
1	2	3	4	5

How hard would it be for a competitor to match your offer?

Very easy Impossible

1 2 3 4 5

Would potential customers see you as innovative and different?

Not at all Completely

1 2 3 4 5

Are local initiatives and decision-making encouraged?

Not at all Completely

1 2 3 4 5

How much do you know about how the needs of your customers might be changing?

Nothing Everything

1 2 3 4 5

What evidence do you have that market and customer evidence gathered every day by employees is collected and acted upon by the organization as a whole?

None at all A lot

1 2 3 4 5

Is there a sense of shared vision and an openness in which challenge and questioning is encouraged? (Do you have evidence that the front-line feel this?)

None at all A lot

1 2 3 4 5

To what extent do employees feel able to contribute all their talents and energy?

Not at all Completely

1 2 3 4 5

More energy goes into maintaining the systems of the organization than meeting customer needs.

True False

1 2 3 4 5

It would be very difficult rapidly to change the way the organization works to meet a market opportunity.

True				False
1	2	3	4	5

Would the hidden structures, the power blocks and empires usually have to be overcome for rapid response to occur?

Not at all			Completely	
1	2	3	4	5

Scores below 30 suggest that your organization may be operating in a relatively low-energy environment; even if you have scores higher than this, you might already have spotted one or two weaker areas.

REFERENCES

1. Welch, J F, Fresco, P and Opie, J D (1995) To our shareowners, *General Electric Annual Report.*
2. Kirkpatrick, D (1998) These days everybody needs a Microsoft strategy, *Fortune*, Time Inc., 12 January.
3. Trapp, R (Sept/Oct 1996) 3M's creative hot house, *Human Resources.*
4. Porter, M (Nov/Dec 1996) What is strategy?, *Harvard Business Review*, **74**, (6).
5. Emmett, S (1998) Branson banks on a quiet lift off, *The Times*, 10 January.
6. Kim, W C and Mauborgne, R (Jan/Feb 1997) Value innovation: the strategic logic of high growth, *Harvard Business Review*, **75**, (1).
7. Duncan, T and Moriarty, S (1997) *Driving Brand Value*, McGraw-Hill, New York.
8. Porter, M (Nov/Dec 1996) What is strategy?, *Harvard Business Review*, **74**, (6).
9. Levin, R (1993) *Complexity: Life at the edge of chaos*, Orion, London.

CHAPTER 4

THE RENAISSANCE WORKFORCE: NEW EXPECTATIONS

SO FAR, we have looked at the virtuous energy cycle from the top-down organizational and market perspectives. There is another energy input into the cycle – the enhanced contribution from those individuals who are employed by an organization. The two aspects to this contribution are the form that this energy needs to take, and the means by which individuals can be encouraged to contribute in this way. These are dealt with in the following two chapters respectively.

My friend and colleague Hugo Pound has a phrase for it: 'organizations need players', that is to say, individuals with a positive attitude and high energy. Chapter 5 will provide insights into the conditions that might produce players; this chapter will focus on the definition of 'being a player'.

Commitment and Context

This chapter addresses two important questions:

- What will organizations need to expect from those who work for them?
- What is meant by energy, at an individual level of analysis?

In the past, it was quite straightforward. The expectation was that an employee would fulfil the requirements of a job description and, if he or she was committed, would demonstrate loyalty to the organization by being prepared to work hard, and by not leaving unless asked to. The situation has changed radically. Increasingly, organizations will need employees who bring much more to their work than simple compliance and effort.

Compliance does not suffice in a work context that increasingly requires high levels of personal decision-making, and occasional risk-taking. Nor will it suffice when the rate of change has made the old formal structures redundant; individuals in the future will be involved, at least in part, in determining their own contribution. This will be particularly relevant as organizations create teams as their fundamental structure, and volatility means that individuals are not only in more than one team, but also move between teams quite frequently. Finally, compliance is unlikely to deliver the value-adding and enterprising behaviours that an organization will require if it is to achieve a competitive advantage, and build a high-energy relationship with its market-place.

Organizations need to understand commitment in a new way. In the future, commitment should not be measured by the length of time an employee spends with an organization, but by the breadth and depth of their individuality, which is reflected in the talents, expertise, resilience and resourcefulness they are prepared to bring to an organization.

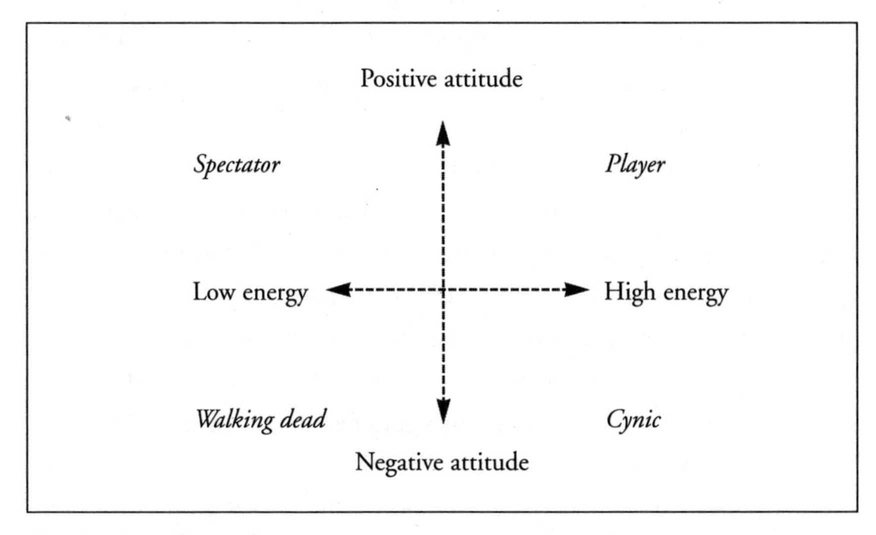

Fig. 4.1 Pound's people positions

The real question, of course, is what will make the players to whom Pound refers (see Fig. 4.1) effective. It is likely that they will need to be innovative, flexible and resourceful decision-makers. It has been suggested that they will need to be multi-skilled, but, given the rate of change in organizations, perhaps it would be more useful to describe them as compulsive learners. However, to answer the question in more detail, it is useful to understand more fully how an individual contributes to an organization.

CONTRIBUTING

Individuals within Renaissance Organizations will need to be able to focus their attention in three ways:

- work process contribution;
- functional specialism; and
- personal contribution development.

The work process contribution could be the development, manufacture and sale of a particular product or service, or particular market niche or locality, characterized by a customer-driven focus. Within this context, an individual will not be contributing purely on the basis of his or her technical expertise, but in other ways as well. In the past, this might have been in terms of some supervisory or managerial contribution, but increasingly today it is as part of a cross-functional team. The collective aim is to meet customer needs in the most value-adding ways.

The fact that work contribution for more and more individuals will be as part of a team or more than one team has already been highlighted. The ability to work well in teams – flexibly adapting a contribution to meet the needs of that particular team – will be very important. The same individual may find himself the leader of one team, a committed follower in another, and an expert who acts as a consultant in a third. Working in teams in this way will require each individual to remain an autonomous agent, and at the same time to sublimate his or her individual needs for the greater good.

Individuals will also often remain contributing in terms of their individual functional specialism, such as marketing or finance, sometimes taking a coaching role to pass on their expertise.

As traditional clarity of responsibility through a single line manager is broken, individuals begin to act with a greater degree of independence and initiative, reconciling conflicting demands, and building linkages, not just within their direct sphere of work but also across the business. Personal contribution will be about developing not just the technical or functional skills within a particular area, but also the behaviours and skills that will make an individual's contribution in the first two areas count. To do this, individuals will need to focus on two overlapping areas in which they need to develop high levels of confidence: the ability to build a whole, interconnected array of relationships; and the ability to make a contribution in a way that is recognized as enterprising.

Connections: building a more enterprising work contribution

I was asked to consider this issue in some work I was doing for a large manufacturing organization. They were going through a major supply-chain re-engineering project; people were to be asked to survive and thrive in a totally different environment, which was to be customer-led rather than production-led. Many of the issues discussed in this book – matrix management, the need for autonomy and integration at the same time, boundary-less behaviour, cross-functional team-working, greater levels of innovation and problem-solving – were involved in this change.

Unlike many organizations, the company acknowledged that the ability of the individuals and teams involved to identify and adapt to a new way of working was crucial to the success of the re-engineering project. My role was to support people within these teams, some of whom controlled budgets of over £60 million, to identify how they were going to work, and to establish the behaviours that would be required if the change was to be successfully implemented. The question was what the key agenda of managers and others in delivering the new strategic goals of the business should be. The aim was to answer the primary question: how were these people going make this thing work? In tackling this, establishing how to re-align the work contributions within the teams, to create a new way of working, was always an important starting point. A significant discovery for the teams was the fact that no one was going to tell them, because nobody else knew either. The outputs were defined, but the best way of achieving them had to be discovered. What was being required was a shift, in the terms described above, from compliance to commitment.

Alongside this, two broad strands of development emerged: first, the break-up of established reporting structures meant that people had to change the way they were dealing with others, and it was important to build up both awareness and skills in this area. The second strand was to identify what might be expected in terms of the individual and collective behaviours that would help participants work more enterprisingly within the new alignment they had created.

EMOTIONAL INTELLIGENCE

These days, much discussion about abilities in the first aspect comes under the heading of 'emotional intelligence'.

In flexibly changing organizations, which are adapting to a volatile market, and in which the notion of role, with its connotations of status and position, becomes increasingly difficult to sustain, the ability to create productive relationships with others will be key. Influence and not authority will be the basis of leadership. This will be underpinned by an understanding of self and of others that is both broad and deep.

A book called *Emotional Intelligence*[1] featured on the bestseller lists in 1997. It was a stimulating review of a wide body of evidence, highlighting the fact that successful individuals (and teams) often seem to be those that demonstrate high levels of emotional intelligence, as opposed to, say, high levels of analytical or technical ability. The latter is important and necessary, but perhaps not enough to guarantee success at work. The book's author Daniel Goleman outlines five aspects of emotional intelligence:

- knowing one's emotions – self-awareness;
- managing emotions – being able to influence one's own emotional states;
- motivating oneself – being able to build personal goals and commitment;
- recognizing emotions in others – understanding the impact of events on others;

- handling relationships – people who have skill and competence here do well in anything that involves interacting with others.

NETWORKING

A key area for personal contribution within a modern organization will be the ability of individuals to use their emotional intelligence to create effective networks. Networks are critical for organizations, and usually thought of as valuable for an individual – they are the conduits through which vital information often flows, and essential for responsiveness. People who are in touch with each other are much more likely to respond with help, resources, information, and so on. I once worked out, with a group of managers I was working with, that the response to a call from someone within a network was one to two days quicker than the response to someone who was unknown. Given the complexity and level of change within today's organization, it seems that networking is the fundamental skill and behaviour upon which a successful contribution will be based. Networking is an act of faith; if you approach it from the point of view of what another can do for you, it is rarely successful. Instead, building networks starts with creating a rapport with many others, and finding ways in which *you* can help *them*. It is very much in the spirit of Renaissance Management, since it is about making connections between other people, and not just with yourself. (For more detail on networks, see Chapter 7.)

This idea of networking is similar to the concept of 'collective individualism' suggested by Colin Hastings.[2] He has looked at the need to develop networks within and between organizations. Looking at the role of knowledge workers, he suggests that they need to be able to create a web of informal linkages, both internal and external to an organization, to gain the information, support and other resources they need. These networks, because of their randomness and potential for the unplanned meeting of ideas, are fertile grounds for the creativity and innovation that is vital. They are also important points at which small but significant changes in the market-place can be identified. The skills and behaviours required of successful networkers will not be about tit for tat exchange, but about being able to create a much more open sharing of thoughts and ideas.

Organizations may increasingly be looking for this boundary-less behaviour internally, and have an increasing expectation that employees will have the skills and the attitudes to exhibit such behaviour. The discomfort will come with external networking. Many organizations talk about creating a much more outward-facing workforce that is in touch, not just with its customers, but also with others, and even possibly with competitors. The question is how prepared they are really to countenance this and resource it. Those that do will have to balance a possible loss of company information against the gains it might make through greater market, customer and innovation sensitivity. A key expectation of employers will therefore be that employees will be able to manage the paradox of openness, trust-building and relationship-building combined with the need to protect the intellectual and commercial property of the organization. To be able do this, of course, the employees will have to be very clear about, and involved with the organization's strategy.

A NEW WAY OF WORKING – A FOCUS ON ENTERPRISE

The rise of individuality as a key focus of organizations is intimately connected with establishing a more productive alignment with the market-place. This will mean that, at an individual level, people will be expected to be more enterprising. Being 'enterprising' consists of a number of disparate elements, as well as aspects of emotional intelligence such as resilience, networking and influence.

Is there any way of capturing all these different elements together into a framework that will allow a Renaissance Organization to focus on how it can best define its expectations of enterprise within this emerging working environment?

Clarification of this might be helped by using a practical model of what constitutes a personal agenda for enterprise. This model has been developed by line managers and academics in the UK, working through an organization called The Research Initiative (TRI). Building on studies of enterprise and entrepreneurship undertaken throughout the world, and ongoing research in the UK, they have developed a pragmatic profile of the attitudes, styles and behaviours of a person who could, in some sense, be described as enterprising. The researchers see it as an energy model, which may be summarized in Fig. 4.2. This model has three levels and they have developed a questionnaire called BASIS, which can be used to profile individual managers against the three levels: energy, direction and skills/behaviours.

The three-level model suggests that, to be enterprising, people will have to possess high levels of energy. It proposes that this might come from three sources: a need for achievement, a sense of being in control of one's own destiny, and a need for autonomy. For many years, a need for achievement has been known as a key factor in how successful a person is likely to be. Notwithstanding the value of creating an

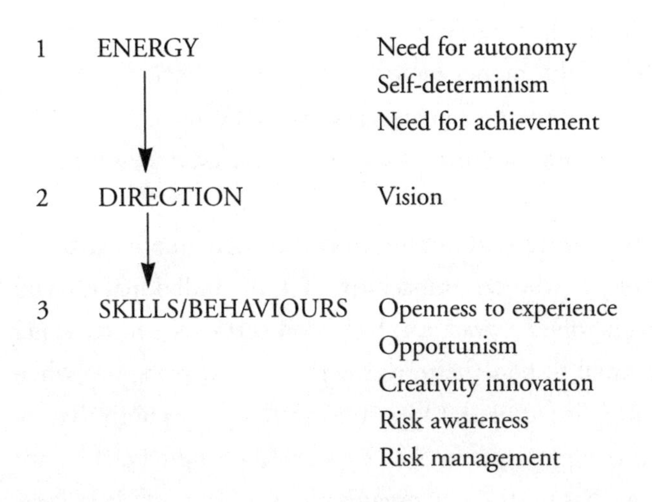

Fig. 4.2 Levels of enterprise on the BASIS model (The Research Initiative[3])

environment at work in which people are not just motivated by goal-oriented personal success, an organization needs a significant number of employees with the desire to make it succeed.

The second source of energy is the belief that each individual can make a difference, that success or failure is generally more related to each individual's activities and abilities than to the influence of others, the environment or luck. In the model, this is termed 'self-determinism', and in many studies it has proved to be an important factor in determining the level at which an individual contributes to change, and the way in which he or she does this.

The third source of energy tapped by 'enterprising' individuals is a need for autonomy. People with a high need for autonomy want to take responsibility for setting their own goals and agenda with their organization. They are happy at times to challenge the status quo and hold out for a new way of doing things.

The second level of the BASIS enterprise model looks at vision. This is more than just having a goal or an objective – it is a sense of the future, a sense of how a particular service or product might flourish in the market, and a sense of how the organization will have to be structured in order to deliver this. According to TRI, vision is not static, but something more dynamic and flexible, responding to new information and change, but still focused on a destination.

The third level of the model looks at five core behaviours that are claimed to contribute to successful enterprise. These are openness to experience, opportunism, innovation and creativity, risk awareness and risk management.

Openness to experience is about an individual being connected to a wide network of others who can impact on what that individual is trying to achieve. It also involves a practical, hands-on sort of learning, which enables the individual to benefit from experience, and recognize where more formal learning is required. Opportunism recognizes both that the market-place is a complex system that is essentially unpredictable, and the impact that this has on the way organizations must work. It is about responsiveness and flexibility, and the ability to move quickly. Creativity and innovation have already been highlighted as key, but the counterbalance to this will probably be the requirement for an ability both to recognize potential consequences of actions and decisions (risk awareness), and also the confidence that there is a broad range of strategies to manage this risk (risk management).

The model does not claim to be totally inclusive but, alongside emotional intelligence and other issues highlighted in this chapter, it represents a starting point for organizations. Using it will enable them to describe more clearly what they will expect from their employees, as the impact of the changes they face becomes apparent. An organization could not or should not expect everyone to score highly in all areas, but most organizations will want evidence of reasonably high scores among their employees. It is important to note that these descriptions of enterprise are not about dimensions of personality or ability, but about style and behaviour, both of which are open to change and development.

CONNECTIONS: ENTERPRISING MANAGEMENT

Using BASIS in several organizations, two dimensions – the need for autonomy, and self-determinism – seem to get consistently low scores. It could be argued that this result might be expected in corporate and still largely hierarchical organizations. Independent action has been, and still is, viewed with some suspicion in many organizations, and the need for it is sometimes suppressed. Where self-determinism scores are low, it is likely that those who feel that they have little control over their destiny, and that they have only modest influence, have felt this since joining the organization.

One indication of whether an organization is starting to become more enterprising would be an increase in its people's reported needs for autonomy and belief in self-determinism.

Fig. 4.3 shows a profile of high-fliers – identified as such by their organizations, not by BASIS – compared to the organization average.

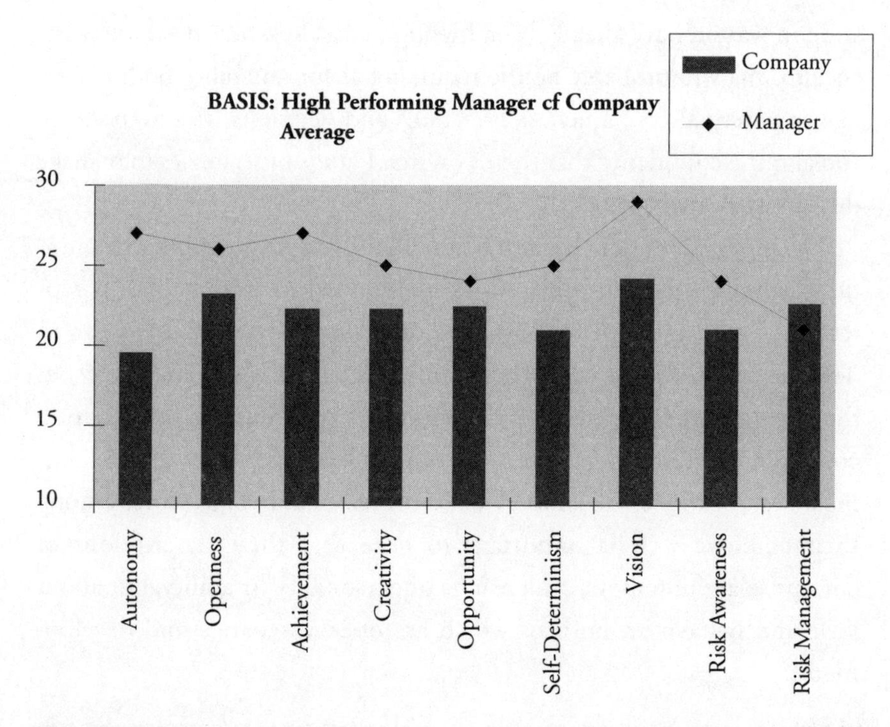

Fig. 4.3 High-flier profile

MOTIVATING A NEW WAY OF WORKING

As already discussed, effective contribution at work in the future will require much more, in most cases, than technical or professional skills. The way people work will also be vital – particularly when they are members of cross-functional teams – as will their ability continually to develop their interpersonal and enterprise abilities. Given these ambitious requirements, the following question still remains: how do you motivate a workforce to behave in this way? A need for achievement will certainly provide an impetus for many, but it is necessary to understand what achievement might mean for someone who has little or no hope of promotion, or of a dramatic salary increase. Furthermore, does the need for achievement encourage the creativity, concern for others, building of rapport etc that are also critical? Further, only a naïve organization does not recognize the tensions and contradictions in the demands outlined here. This involves not only individual versus team considerations, but also how an organization can allow the space for creativity and experimentation, and still focus on achieving goals; how it can encourage people to respond to opportunities, but not lose sight of the overall vision; how it can focus on goals and build a network?

These matters are the central concern of the next chapter.

Connections: enterprise in the front line at the Royal Mail

My colleague David Brech was Marketing Director with the Royal Mail during a remarkable period of turnaround. In the mid-1980s, the organization accounted for nearly half the days lost to strikes in the UK, yet, by the early 1990s, it was generally held to be the most effective and profitable of its type in Europe. Brech is able to provide excellent examples of the enterprise potential of even the most junior front-line staff during this period.

The Royal Mail created a framework of small business units with great powers of autonomy, and provided management information systems to allow them to get feedback on progress against key criteria, and to empower local decision-making. A good example was a team of telephonists in the Newcastle customer care department. They noticed that a group of small businesses on a far-distant trading estate was forced to accept a last collection of the day at 2pm. This meant that much of their correspondence had to wait until the following day, losing them a day's cash flow on billing, and delaying urgent orders and responses.

Under the past system, the response to this might have been

simply to shrug shoulders – someone else would have had to have done without their 5pm pick-up if the Royal Mail tried to meet this need. However, this customer care team worked out a win/win solution. They found another collection van that was finishing its round at 5pm some 10 miles away. They negotiated with the small businesses, and it was agreed that, if they could bring their urgent mail on the estate to a common point for 5pm, this van would divert to make a pick-up. Along with other initiatives, this contributed to a rapid improvement in the teams' customer satisfaction ratings, which were regularly measured. All this was achieved without the 'benefit' of a manager.

In Manchester, a similar customer care team noticed that, if small sums of cash were lost in the post, the standard procedure was to spend days investigating the route from posting point to delivery point. The customer suffered not only the loss, but, subsequently, also the delay of investigation, and eventually received a lawyer's letter disclaiming responsibility.

The Manchester team proposed instant cash settlements, and, having constructed an audit trail, they proved that these ex gratia payments paid back their investment many times in saved administrative costs. As a bonus, the customers were delighted.

The common thread is that the Royal Mail provided the front-line staff with the toolkit to make a simple business case. Without this, staff initiative came across as a lightweight request for more resources, with little accountability for outcomes or return on investment. Given the means and the authority, the front line was able to demonstrate that it is closer to the detail than managers, and is highly motivated to create energy-saving customer-oriented solutions.

REFERENCES

1. Goleman, D (1996) *Emotional Intelligence*, Bloomsbury, London.
2. Hastings, C (1993) *The New Organization*, McGraw-Hill, Maidenhead.
3. TRI (1996) *The BASIS Manual*, The Research Initiative, Ware.

CHAPTER 5

MOTIVATING AND ENERGIZING A RENAISSANCE WORKFORCE

CHAPTER 4 has outlined the broad expectations that an organization may have of its employees, if it wants to become better aligned with the needs of the rest of its stakeholders.

These expectations relate to individual behaviour within an organization, but what about the management approach that will encourage individuals to behave in a certain way? It could be argued that having a set of expectations, and encouraging people to behave accordingly, will be motivating enough. There is some truth in this, but it is important to ask a deeper question about why it should be so. Answering the question allows managers both to broaden the impact, in order to involve those who might not otherwise be switched on by these new expectations, and to manage performance better, in order to gain the much wider diversity of attitudes, skills and behaviours that will be required.

Organizations need to create the right conditions for each individual to rise to the challenge of defining his or her own role, and seek innovative ways of adding value to their organization. In its quest to do this, an organization needs to consider the way it shapes the contribution of the people who work for it.

CHALLENGING ASSUMPTIONS

How is it possible to get the maximum number of people to contribute a greater amount of energy and talent to the organization? A standard response may be to tinker with the pay and reward system in some way, to try to incentivize a new way of working. (This would assume the goal-based theory of motivation discussed below.) Renaissance Organizations, however, will recognize the limitations of this approach.

All organizations need to challenge the assumptions they have about individuals and motivation if they are seeking to build a high-energy environment. For example, is it true that all individuals are motivated by 'more responsibility', and is it necessarily bad if they are not? There is a real danger of creating literal and psychological 'contracts', on which, in fact, an organization cannot deliver. Can every employee win promotion or a pay increase if they want it? In a world of flatter organizations, where there is much pressure on costs, is this possible? Consider the case of the 53-year-old manager who has reached a plateau, with no possibility of advancement, at the top of his or her pay scale? What is his or her incentive for change and continuous learning? It is little wonder that individuals like these are not motivated; the possible rewards do not apply to them, and they become labelled as 'reactionary', 'stick-in-the-mud', and so on. Even worse, their experience and potential is often discarded.

If it were possible to create an environment in which such people did feel motivated, and wanted to learn and change, would this not be a powerful release of energy into an organization – a potent blend of experience and motivation? Renaissance Management is about finding ways of motivating every employee as far as possible, and recognizes the innate contribution of everyone. 'Performance management' in this perspective needs to take account of the following:

- the diversity of ways in which people are motivated;
- the fact that individuals differ in what motivates them; and
- the fact that what motivates an individual differs over time and may be inconsistent.

At this point, it is useful to make the distinction between extrinsic and intrinsic motivation. Extrinsic motivation is when a person does something in order to achieve something else – the extrinsic motivator. Such motivators might include pay, status, recognition, power, prestige and punishment. Intrinsic motivation occurs when something is done for the sake of itself. Internal motivators can include feelings of being in control and belonging, learning, pleasure, excitement and self-esteem.

Many organizations have a rather narrow view of what motivates and energizes people. It usually focuses on a goal-based approach, relating to extrinsic motivators. Stereotypically, the formula seems to run as follows: give individuals goals based upon organizational objectives and, if possible, tie some rewards in, and you will get the behaviours you want. Many performance management schemes consist of ever more sophisticated ways of manipulating the external rewards. Schemes that offer choices of reward do seem to have an impact, and they probably deliver, some of the time, some of the behaviours an organization needs.

Table 5.1 suggests why this might be so.

CONNECTIONS: WHAT EMPLOYEES EXPECT FROM COMPANIES[1]

The Conference Board, a business research organization, undertook a survey of 92 organizations (two-thirds US-based, the rest mainly European), to explore what employees really wanted from organizations. The results reveal a major change in emphasis, which organizations will struggle to meet.

Table 5.1 What employees want from an organization

Per cent of employees asked	Extremely important	Important
Interesting, challenging work	54	33
Open, two-way communication	53	27
Tools, opportunities for growth and development	30	47
Realistic performance management	23	44
Secure employment	27	34
Work/life balance	15	40
Involvement in decision-making	20	35
Performance-based pay	16	35
Equitable benefits	10	29
Non-monetary rewards and recognition	9	30
Portable pensions	4	10
Other	4	1

Motivating the heart

Table 5.1 reveals the real limitations to goal-based approaches to motivation. Intrinsic motivators such as interesting work, being listened to (communication), and growth and development comprise the top three things people want from work. Moreover, even the best performance management systems based upon extrinsic rewards encounter problems of fairness and manipulation; in addition, there is often the perception among employees that 'this is just a sophisticated way of controlling us'.

Anyway, do organizations want only motivation that is focused on achieving goals? An over-emphasis on goals emphasizes compliance and conformity, and does not encourage challenge or experimentation. Furthermore, it does not in itself lead to support for others; in fact, if others' needs are not seen as encompassed within the goals a particular person is facing, then it may positively discourage it.

If it is to earn a high-energy contribution, Renaissance Management needs to search beyond extrinsic motivators and tap into things that are at the heart of what it is to be human. Consider the case of Rico Medellin, where there is something far more potent and subtle than the pursuit of reward going on:

> *He works on an assembly line. The task he has to perform on each unit that passes in front of his station should take 43 seconds to perform – the exact same operation almost six hundred times a day. Most people would grow tired of such work very soon, but Rico has been at this job for over five years, and he still enjoys it. The reason is because he approaches his task in the same way an Olympic athlete approaches his event. He is always asking himself how he can beat his record. Like a runner who has trained for years to shave a few seconds off his best performance on the track, Rico has trained himself to better his time on the assembly line. With the painstaking care of a surgeon, he has worked out a private routine for how to use his tools, and how to do his moves. After five years, his best average for a day has been twenty-eight seconds per unit. In part he tries to improve his performance in order to earn a bonus and the respect of his supervisors, but most often he does not even tell others that he is ahead, and lets his success go unnoticed. It is enough for him to know that he can do it, and when he is working at top performance the experience is so enthralling that it is almost painful for him to slow down.*

Rico is experiencing what Hungarian-born American psychologist Mihaly Csikmentmihalyi would call 'flow'.[2] Csikmentmihalyi has established that the following conditions are important for flow:

- clear goals – intrinsic to the activity itself, not external to it, such as a reward or punishment;
- immediate feedback – people know all the time how well they are doing;

- skill/challenge match – activities that stretch but do not go beyond an individual's capabilities;
- a sense of control – individuals need to feel that potentially they are in control of what they do – free from the arbitrary intervention of outside forces. Importantly this means that there is a possibility of control rather than whether it exists at a particular time or circumstance eg in playing tennis there is the possibility of being able to accurately control the ball, whether or not you are able to do so on a particular shot.

Rico has discovered a way to develop extraordinary commitment and energy, to gain intrinsic pleasure from what seems the most mundane of jobs. Flow is a phenomenon that Csikmentmihalyi has discovered as part of the work experience of people in all walks of life, from surgeons to peasant farmers. It occurs when someone is so immersed in what they are doing that they feel a sense of exhilaration, of control, and of time standing still. When this state of mind is achieved, work becomes a profound experience.

Not everyone is able to become so fanatically devoted to work, and bring so much energy to it. The question needs to be asked: how does an organization even begin to develop this level of energy and commitment in its employees? Fortunately, perhaps, flow is not the whole of intrinsic motivation, just a special expression of it. Several organizations are starting to design themselves as places in which employees can experience a high level of intrinsic motivation, with resultant high levels of productivity and flexibility. Such organizations have emphasized a variety of aspects of intrinsic motivation, but there are several common threads:

- an emphasis on mastery, ie individuals feeling in control, expressed either as a higher level of autonomy, or individual development;
- an emphasis on openness, trust and involvement with co-operative and supportive groupings;
- a focus on the individual, and a responsiveness to individual needs;
- an environment that allows for fun and experimentation.

These requirements are another example of a virtuous energy cycle. Encouraging mastery, an open and exciting environment, and feeling of concern and respect for the individual, not only makes people feel more motivated and energized, it encourages the display of organizationally useful behaviours. For example, research on creativity suggests that it will rarely occur in situations of goal-focused, deal-line obsessed anxiety. It is much more likely in an environment of openness, experimentation, calculated risk, and even fun!

CONNECTIONS: MANAGING TO HAVE FUN

Matt Weinstein[3] runs a consultancy in the US called Playfair. Its focus is a technology aimed at helping over 400 organizations to build successful teams using laughter, fun and play. It claims that the 'intentional use of fun on the job can help improve employee morale, heighten productivity, create a more people-centred corporate culture and, ultimately, increase profitability'. Weinstein strongly argues that work and play should not be regarded as opposites if an organization is to achieve its full potential.

Certainly, organizations that have emphasized intrinsic motivation based on either form of mastery have seen significant organizational benefits. For example, the Apex Group Inc., a provider of software engineering and network and systems integration, has managed to achieve far lower rates of staff turnover than the industry average, which is notoriously high. The personal continuity it can thereby maintain benefits the organization through critical strategic alliances with some of the industries' big players, including Microsoft, Hewlett-Packard and Oracle.[4] This has been achieved by creating an individualized, accredited personal-development route for the employees, which emphasizes the breadth and depth of the skills required in the industry. Using an intensive mixture of mentoring, internal and external developed programmes, and encouraging more informal learning, individuals achieve certificated badges of achievement across a variety of technologies and disciplines. As a result of this, Apex has built an environment in which motivation is 'palpable', and the company therefore has a real competitive edge.

Apex is a small organization of about 180 employees, but strategies to improve the level of intrinsic motivation are not limited to smaller organizations. The Opel Eisenach plant in the former East Germany employs over 2,000 people, and is the most productive car plant in Europe. It was set up on the site of an old Communist car-production facility as a test-bed for a new way of working within Opel. The plant is based upon highly flexible team-working, with each team having full responsibility for its area of work. Management's role is as coach and advisor. Flexibility is developed not just within teams but between teams, with inter-team exchanges to enable everyone to see the big picture. People are given the opportunity to challenge all work procedures, restructure work-flow, and make efficiencies, which could include improvements to materials, assembly methods, or equipment. Learning is both encouraged and rewarded, and a culture of open communications and trust is promoted. In fact, the inherent intrinsic motivation is actively built up in virtually every respect, and covers all four themes identified above.

Haasen and Shea,[5] in analysing the motivational environment of the plant, have concluded that

> *by far the most important message from Opel Eisenach's short history is that there is no limit to people's productivity. Opel Eisenach's secret of success is a team concept that provides an environment of integration and mutual support. Being part of a small family and working with friends is enjoyable... the outcome is unusual productivity. In early February of 1996, Opel Eisenach reported that it had produced 160,000 vehicles in 1995, an incredible 20% increase over 1994.*

CONNECTIONS: SEMCO

Perhaps the best-known example of an organization that has emphasized the potential of the intrinsic motivation of a workforce is that of Semco, a Brazilian manufacturer of marine and food-processing machinery. This company grew elevenfold in the late 1980s and early 1990s, during a time of deep recession in Brazil. Ricardo Semler,[6] its famous CEO, has created a somewhat unusual organization, in which

- there are almost no manuals and written procedures;
- workers make the decisions previously made by management;
- employees are treated as responsible adults;
- most employees set their own working hours;
- all employees have access to the company books;
- all employees vote on important company decisions; and
- most managerial staff set their own salaries and bonuses.

There is a growing body of anecdotal evidence of the galvanizing effect that this degree of focus on intrinsic motivation can have on an organization, although the implementation of changes to increase levels of intrinsic motivation can be problematic. In the past, research in such areas as job enrichment (making jobs intrinsically more interesting) has shown that establishing these approaches can have positive effects on a range of performance measures.

There is a danger, however, in mimicking what others have done. A 'one size fits all' approach, which blindly introduces teams, individual development, and more autonomous working, will not be successful just because it has worked elsewhere. Not all changes will motivate all people equally.

Reversal Theory

So far, the way of creating complex motivational environments that encourage the essentially paradoxical behaviours suggested in Chapter 2 (ie focus and experimentation, conformity and challenge, team play and individual action) has not been addressed. Nor has the way an organization can structure its motivational options and allow for diversity. Reversal Theory, a theory of motivation that has already proved useful in the areas of sports and health psychology, is starting to have an impact on the world of organizations, and may begin to address some of these issues. It provides a powerful framework, within which strategies based upon both intrinsic and extrinsic motivation can be accommodated, and allows organizations to understand the differences that lie between individuals in the way they are motivated.

The theory's prime author is Professor Michael Apter, a British psychologist working at the University of Georgetown, Washington.[7] His work recognizes and focuses on the paradoxes of human behaviour and suggests that we are all

- motivated to be serious and pursue goals, but are also motivated to play, take risks and look for excitement;
- motivated to conform but also motivated to challenge;
- motivated by issues to do with mastery – not just of people, but also of processes and ideas – but also by caring, friendship and affection; and
- motivated by interest and focus on ourselves, but also on others.

Each of these statements encapsulates two motivational states, or 'ways of being' (see Fig. 5.1). A person's 'state' is the way that person views the world, or particular aspects of it; he or she may at different times see the same activity in quite different ways. Sometimes a person may feel motivated in a particular situation because it will give them access to some other goal, such as a pay rise; sometimes because it enables them to work with people they like; sometimes because it will allow them to prove a point or challenge the system; sometimes just simply because they find the activity interesting and fulfilling. The important factor is that the activity or situation has stayed the same but the response to it has changed because the motivational state has changed. Specifically, these eight states can be recognized as four pairs of opposites. People switch – or 'reverse' – fairly frequently between these opposite 'motivational states' in the course of everyday life and under a variety of circumstances.

The pairs of states (as shown in Fig. 5.1) are as follows:

- The serious (goal-oriented) state, focused on important goals, planning ahead, avoiding surprises and anxiety, versus the playful (means-oriented) state, focused on immediate enjoyment, acting spontaneously, creating excitement and taking risks.
- The compliant (conformist) state, focused on obligations and the maintenance of rules and routines, versus the challenging (negativistic) state, a questioning, assumption-testing state focused on personal freedom.

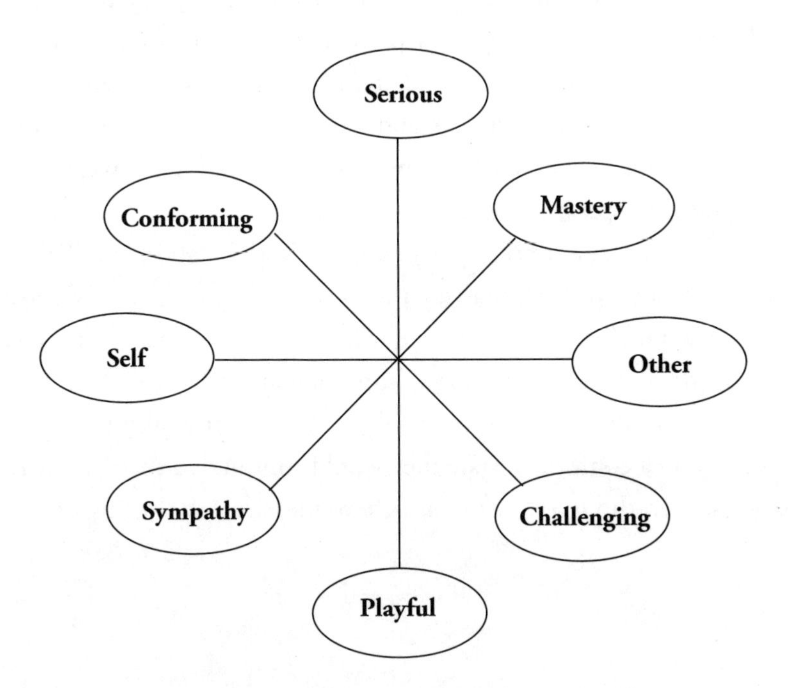

Fig. 5.1 Pairs of motivational states

- The mastery state, focused on power, control and dominance, versus the sympathy state, focused on security, caring and harmony.
- The self-centred state, focused on one's own needs, versus the other-centred state, focused on the needs of others.

These states combine with each other in various ways at different times, to give rise to the full range of human emotions and behaviours.

These states are experienced not singly but in combinations of one of each pair, although one or two will be ascendant at any one time. An important argument of Reversal Theory is that all eight states contribute to mental health, and that a person needs to become skilful in meeting the different needs of those states through his or her behaviour and activities. Importantly, virtually all combinations of the states can drive organizationally useful behaviours (see Table 5.2).

It should now be possible to recognize how successful organizations have built their motivational environments. Clearly, both Apex and Opel have emphasized environments that encourage self-oriented mastery. The team-working at Opel, in particular, taps into the sympathy states, in terms of the family atmosphere. Motivations to challenge and question will also be encouraged and not driven underground into 'political' behaviour. The management-for-fun ideas of Matt Weinstein relate to meeting people's needs in the playful/means-oriented state ('flow' is probably an example of high arousal in this state). The Reversal Theory model also emphasizes the place of extrinsic motivators. People in a serious/goal-oriented state will find the existence of specific objectives, and rewards of some kind, important and valuable. (NB: they would not be motivated by these while they were in a playful state.) Interestingly, in a conformist state they would continue to work towards those goals, even though they might believe they were the wrong ones.

Table 5.2 Contribution of motivational states to organizational energy

Motivational state	Experienced at work as:
Goal-oriented (serious)	Focus on goals, achievement, direction, planning – risk-conscious. Serious.
Means-oriented (playful)	Focus on experimenting, trying things out, creativity, open thinking, intrinsic pleasure of the activity or job itself. Playful.
Conformist	Focus on implementation, following agreements and processes. A concern for maintenance, fitting in.
Challenging	Focus on being different, breaking conventions, critical analysis, conflict.
Self-oriented/sympathy	Focus on building harmony and good personal working relations, wanting to belong and co-operate. Wanting to be supported.
Other-oriented/sympathy	Focus on emotionally supporting and caring for others, willingness to sacrifice own needs for others. Team spirit.
Self-oriented/mastery	Focus on personal success and a willingness to take responsibility, control and master new challenges.
Other-oriented/mastery	Wanting the team or the organization to succeed. Focus on building up the power and resources of others.

THE IMPACT OF WORK

The implications of the Reversal Theory are interesting. According to Apter, who draws on a wide variety of diverse ethnic and cultural research, everyone experiences all of the eight states, differing in the amount of time they spend in each of them. The result of this is that organizations should not rely on just one motivational approach.

All eight states contribute to a high-performance motivational environment. Every motivational state also has something distinctive and essential of its own to contribute. Traditionally, organizations (and teams) tend to emphasize the serious, compliant and mastery motivational states, at the expense of the playful, challenging and sympathy states. It could be argued that, if organizations encourage only a limited range of states – perhaps about half – then they should not be disappointed if they only get one half of a person's personality and contribution. Among other problems, a limited involvement of the whole of an individual makes change and innovation more difficult to accomplish and to sustain; change will involve risk, challenge, and support for many others. Renaissance Organizations will capture the potential of their employees by giving great attention to the range of motivational opportunities they provide, across all eight states.

Reversal Theory allows us the mapping of the contribution that diversity can make at two levels. The first level relates to the diverse environment, in which the organizationally relevant behaviours elicited by each motivational state can encourage the motivational range of the organization. The second level of diversity exists at the individual level. People differ in the amount of time they spend in each state. Although this is, in part, a function of the climate and culture of an organization (see Connections, below), it is also determined by each person's individual history and the stage of their life. Reversal Theory provides the opportunity both to understand better the contribution this individual diversity offers, and to access the contribution this diversity can make at an individual level.

Using this theory, it is possible to approach the case of the manager who has reached a plateau with renewed insights into the cause of his or her low-energy contribution. It will also allow the possibility of making interventions across all the motivational states to improve that contribution. (This will be an example of the new 'psychological contract'.)

BUILDING A MOTIVATIONALLY RICH ENVIRONMENT

A focus on Reversal Theory is useful because it offers a framework for understanding and improving the motivational climate of work, which accommodates all the insights and innovations in this area over the last thirty years. In addition, it goes beyond other current theories, and allows organizations to understand the essential inconsistency of individuals and the potential that such inconsistency offers an organization. People can and do work in the paradoxical way proposed in Chapter 2, because that is how they experience life as a whole.

The first step for any organization wishing to create a richer, more intrinsically motivating environment will be to understand better the organization's current environment. An important factor will be to understand the gap between what is wanted by individuals and what they are receiving. Recently, a relatively simple survey by Gallup[8] has shown the impact of a satisfied workforce: organizations in which employees responded highly in terms of satisfaction in such areas as clear goals, recognition, support, friendship and learning, out-performed rivals in terms of hard measures such as productivity (by 22 per cent), customer satisfaction (38 per cent), profitability (27 per cent), and employee retention (22 per cent). (All figures are from the US.)

However, it is possible to go a stage beyond this. Knowing that employees are happy is important, but it is vital to know what they think is motivationally important. For example, having decided to exercise their playful and challenge states outside a work environment, a satisfied workforce may not reveal that challenge and creativity are not regarded as important. It also essential to be clear whether there are any differences between managers and the rest of the workforce over what is considered to be important. Major blockages can occur when, for example, the senior team and the workforce think that it is important to be motivated to take more responsibility and act autonomously, but middle managers disagree!

There are ways of profiling the motivational environment of an organization (see Connections, below). However, it is also important that the management of the organization is deeply and thoughtfully in touch with the way in which different parts and individuals within the organization are presently motivated, and to what extent they feel satisfied within different motivational states. A key element of building high-performing teams will be the extent to which a wide variety of motivational states are promoted, and satisfaction can be achieved within them. Other critical circumstances for understanding and managing the motivational environment would be situations of restructuring, merger, takeover, and so on.

CONNECTIONS – WORK IMPACT

The Apter Work Impact System[9] is an instrument based on Reversal Theory, which surveys the motivational states as organizational values, and tackles these issues. Ongoing work has shown that individuals within organizations find that their needs within different states are met to different extents. Not surprisingly, personal power (self-oriented mastery) and challenge are among the least satisfied states (see Fig. 5.2). This part of the survey shows an individual comparison of what a group of employees consider to be important, and the extent to which they feel satisfied in these states. The system has also demonstrated that different parts of the organization can have quite different levels of importance and satisfaction, particularly among the sub-dimensions that make up different states.

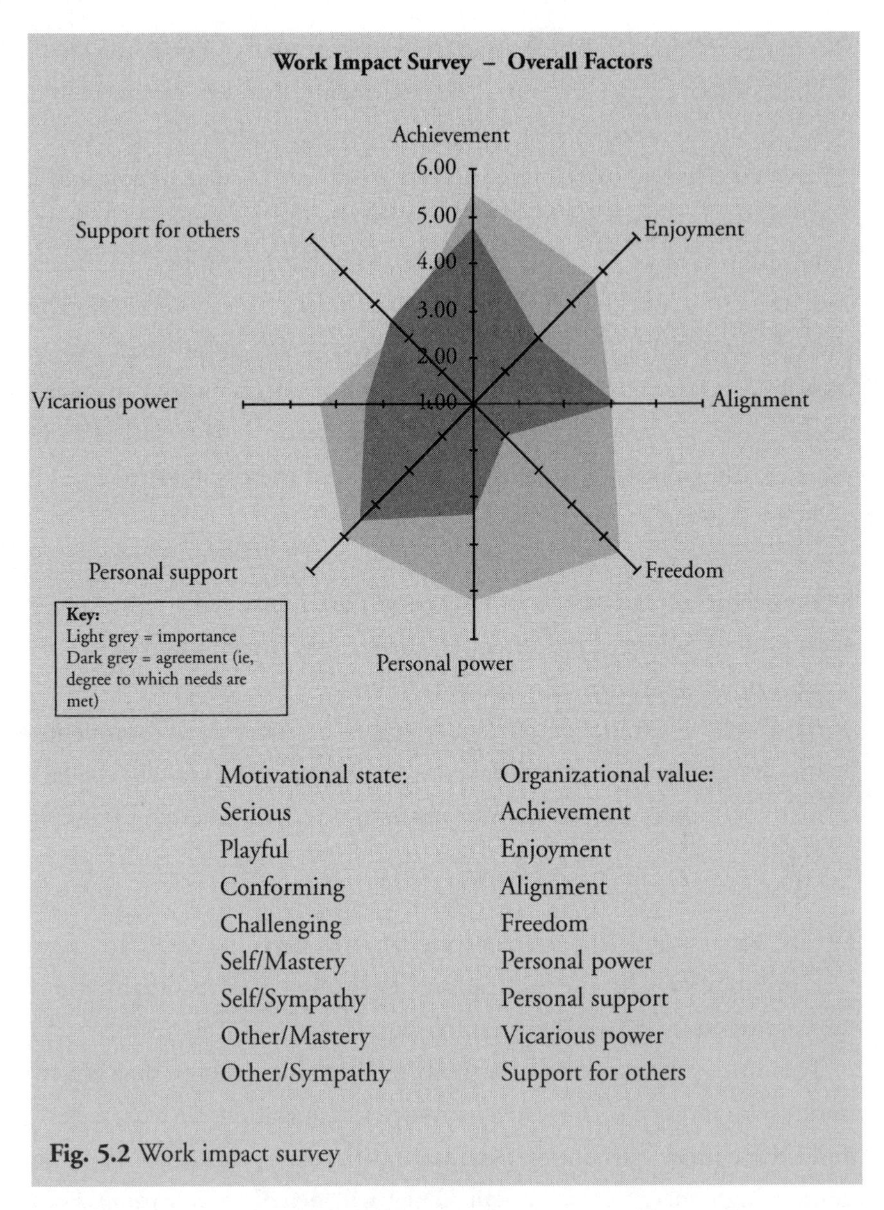

Fig. 5.2 Work impact survey

SUMMARY

This chapter has focused on what is required to build the conditions in which individuals can contribute their full potential to an organization. Organizations need to look beyond the usual mix of carrot and stick.

Somewhat cynically, in the face of a volatile and competitive market, it could be argued that the instinctive organizational response is a knee-jerk reaction of tighter control – of costs, quality, decision-making – and exhortation. This response is locked into an outmoded view of how to achieve an effective workforce, and can result in a climate of fear and a 'head down' mentality, which is just what should be avoided. At best, exhortation seems to result in people working harder but rarely smarter, and leads to a working climate that encourages excessive hours. The strategy does not acknowledge the inherent power in an increasingly mobile workforce, and ignores it in terms of its effects on staff turnover. And it does not begin to start aligning the needs, talents and energy-value creating ability of individuals with that of the organization.

The following are necessary:

- a much greater awareness of how people are motivated;
- an understanding of the potential worth to the organization of people who are more intrinsically motivated; and
- the need to build complex and rich motivational environments, which reflect not just the differences between people, but also the fact that individuals are constantly changing and inconsistent in their needs.

Finally, Renaissance Management will have to keep in touch, at a new level of intensity, with the motivational environment of its organization, responding to its dynamic and unfolding nature.

This brings us back to the virtuous circle of high energy that organizations are trying to achieve. Renaissance Organizations actively seek to build the climate, structures, systems and processes that allow them to build a high-energy environment. They will benefit much more from the potential of their employees, who will have a strong sense of purpose, and believe that innovation, and formulating a response to changes in the market-place, is their responsibility. In the markets in which they operate they will be recognized as being, either through what they offer or the way they offer it, capable of meeting customer needs in ways that set them apart from their potential competitors. Internally, they will have created an architecture, which means that they will be characterized by their responsiveness to change, their efficiency and adaptability. Also noticeable will be their ability to realize the innovative potential, not just within specific groups or individuals, but between the different parts of the organization as a whole. In every sense, a Renaissance Organization is committed to all its stakeholders and aligned to its objectives. If the organization can unlock this commitment, it can build energy from both ends: from its people and from its market-place. Designing and managing an organization that can do this is at the heart of Renaissance Management.

REFERENCES

1. Implementing the new employment compact, *HR Executive Review*, The Conference Board – reported in the *Financial Times*, 25 April 1997.
2. Csikmentmihalyi, M (1992) *The Psychology of Happiness*, Rider, London.
3. Weinstein, M (1996) *Managing to Have Fun*, Fireside, New York.
4. Haasen, A and Shea, G F (1997) *A Better Place to Work*, American Management Association, New York.
5. Haasen, A and Shea, G F (1997) ibid.
6. Semler, R (1993) *Maverick!*, Century Random House, London.
7. Apter, M (1989) *Reversal Theory, Motivation, Emotion and Personality*, Routledge, London. Further details of organizational, team and individual profiling can be obtained from Apter International Ltd, The Offices, Glaston Road, Uppingham, Rutland, LE15 9EU, UK, or from Professor Michael Apter PhD, 2539 Oak Valley Drive, Vienna, Virginia VA22181, USA.
8. Caulkin, S (1998) Where that pat on the head can mean money in the bank, *Observer*, 19 April.
9. Carter, S, Apter, M and Shelton, M (1998) *The Apter Work Impact System*, Apter International, Uppingham.

Part

2

CHAPTER 6

DESIGNING AND MANAGING A RENAISSANCE ORGANIZATION

THE HEART OF THE MATTER

AS HAS been argued, a successful response to volatility in the market-place can be achieved by combining two factors – superior market-place alignment (strategic and local), with a deep focus on creating the conditions under which each individual member of the organization can really contribute. Renaissance Management is therefore about maximizing these potentially mutually reinforcing factors. Once there is a detailed understanding of the nature of the relationships between the organization and the market, and between organizations and their individual employees, the next step must be to ask what sort of organization is a Renaissance Organization.

This is the heart of the matter. How is it possible to design and manage an organization that can remain aligned with the needs of the market-place and stakeholders through responsiveness and innovation? How can management create an organization in which individuals can and want to maximally contribute? Furthermore, the architecture of such an organization will have to keep pace with the rate of change in the environment. The implications of this are that organization design will have to allow for constant evolution, which will sometimes be extremely rapid. The organization will also need to be able to resource considerable energy in order to be able to do this.

The following chapters will show how such organizations can be built. This chapter looks at the elements of an organization that allow it to gain energy from the market-place. Chapter 7 looks at the design elements that will help an organization to use that energy efficiently. As flexibility, autonomy and responsiveness will be key components of this, Chapter 8 focuses on the connections that need to be made to maintain the coherence and integrity of the organization.

DESIGNING FOR DIVERSITY AND INTEGRATION

On the face of it, building organizations for maximum flexibility would seem to be an essential design requirement. Such a design would break away from fixed structures and roles, and move towards more responsive arrangements, aligned more closely with the changing business environment. This, at least in part, can be achieved by 'empowering' a more autonomous workforce, which is capable of taking its own decisions and, to an extent, sets its own goals. This has been understood at an organizational level for quite some time; many organizations in the 1980s tried to devolve as much power as possible away from head office to the front line, to enable them to respond quickly to local challenges. It was, and largely still is fashionable to create autonomous business units capable of making a whole range of decisions that could previously only be undertaken at head-office level. In doing this, larger organizations can capture the speed and enterprise of much smaller companies, in which employees can respond directly to market or customer needs, independent of any particular functional pigeon-hole or rigid job description.

Asea Brown Boveri (ABB) is an example of an organization that has created real autonomy within the overall framework of a multi-national company. It has created within this framework around 1,300 independent businesses, further sub-divided into 5,000 autonomous profit centres. It is built up from 'cells' of cross-functional teams, each with about 10 members.

Maximizing flexibility creates problems of its own, however, namely:

- The role of head office and senior management becomes somewhat ambiguous.
- How does the learning and experience in one part of the business get transferred for the benefit of all?
- Flexibility by itself does not guarantee the best fit between an organization's constituent parts and the needs of the market-place.
- If you have a structure of autonomous business units, how do you achieve the economies of scale of a large organization, release the synergy that lies between the different parts of the organization and exploit market share?

Creating a balance between the advantages of flexibility, achieved through empowerment and autonomy, and the need to create coherence and efficiency, through integration, is a key issue in organization design. This is a genuinely problematic area for many businesses and organizations. More than once, serious attempts have been made to create more autonomous work teams, usually focused on a product or locality. Typically, problems of co-ordination and communication have occurred, particularly while everyone tried to establish the implications of this new way of working. It is not uncommon for an organization to underestimate the extent of these changes in behavioural terms. After initial enthusiasm, senior management tend to become nervous as the teams start to work in unpredictable ways or, more accurately, in ways that senior management would not have anticipated, from their own experience. In order to retrieve the situation, which they see as an initiative going out of control, attempts are made to wind back to a more hierarchical – top-down – way of working. The results are frustration, wasted energy and, in some cases, real personal cost.

One challenge for Renaissance architecture, therefore, is to find designs that allow for optimum flexibility and integration at the same time. Another challenge is to capture and deploy the innovative potential of an organization at all levels, from strategic to local.

DESIGNING A RENAISSANCE ORGANIZATION

A fundamental block to creating an organization that can change successfully to meet the realities and opportunities of the market-place lies in the fact that many are locked into a very specific set of expectations about what organizations should be like. Traditionally, the design of organizations has been seen in terms of a number of rational components, including spans of control, roles, lines of communication, hierarchies and formal processes. These ideas have arisen from particular circumstances in which stability and control were seen as realistic possibilities. They represent such a strong perspective that it is very hard to see organizations being created in any other way. However, the drivers for change, and the responses required by organizations (see Chapter 2), suggest that organizations must create new ways of seeing themselves, and new design components.

Creating high-energy Renaissance Organizations will therefore require some designing for forgetting and unplanning – unplanning traditional work processes, forgetting functional demarcation, dismantling highly detailed plans that extend over a time horizon – out of a pocket of predictability and into uncertainty. Incidentally, it is perhaps not unreasonable to suggest that, in organizations that operate in a particularly uncertain environment, this time horizon might be measured in months, not years.

Using the idea of organizations as energy systems is a way of 'letting go' of old ways of seeing organizations. Organizations need to be provoked to see the world differently. The 'provocations' that concluded Chapter 3 may suggest one way of beginning this process.

For many of the organizations in this book it has taken courage and vision to 'unthink' the powerful assumptions that have been developed over time and which have shaped our views of how organizations should be built and run. Often the inspiration has come from the organization's founder – as in the case of Gore-Tex discussed earlier. Without inspiration and courage from the top, organizational design is more likely to follow what everyone has always done rather than what the market needs.

Challenging the way things are currently done in existing organizations is not going to be easy. Organizations that do not have faith in their employees as individuals are going to find it impossible. They might wish to consider the following:

- Does their design inspire their people – what would be the benefits if it did?
- How confident are they that people understand and want what they want – do the communication processes work that well?
- Does the way the organization is designed enhance its brand and market reputation?

Letting go of old assumptions and perspectives on what organizations should be like does not mean, however, that that they should be replaced by other, similarly rigid perspectives. Given that organizations are unique, and face unique challenges and opportunities, there is no such thing as an ideal design. There are, however, a number of insights and elements that organizations can draw from a distillation of the experience and insights of others. These suggest new ways of establishing connectedness and effective energy flow. A decision will need to be made about precisely how these elements will be applied, and the extent to which this will be done, given the limitations of the ability of one organization to learn from another. Organizations will have to adapt the elements to find their own solution. As Peter Martin has indicated (see Connections, below), even the seemingly most out-moded of structures can be found to be relevant and provide highly competitive, high-energy solutions to building sustainability. What is also interesting about his article is that he notes that change itself is a way of re-energizing a business. Could this be because it creates the opportunity for building new relationships, and for removing the blockages to energy flow?

CONNECTIONS: THE CASE FOR CONGLOMERATES

Peter Martin,[1] writing in the *Financial Times*, has pointed out that the hype for focus and break-up is in danger of moving from a business consensus to a dogma. Conglomerates, it is argued, belong to a time when markets were inefficient and resources immobile. They allowed investors to achieve the virtues of portfolio diversification – higher returns with lower risk – in a way that was otherwise difficult. Within such organizations, scarce resources – capital, know-how, managerial talent, political influence – could be applied effectively to a wider collection of businesses. Such times have gone, it is argued; investors no longer need this mechanism, which can be more precisely achieved by other means. What is required is the management focus that only a single business can achieve; without this, resource allocation inside the company will always be less effective than in the wider capital market.

The problem with all this, according to Peter Martin, is that it ignores the fact that there are some very successful conglomerates – he cites Granada in the UK, and General Electric as the most successful company in the US. On the other hand, many single-focus businesses fail.

Martin challenges the notion that the structure of conglomerates inevitably means that decisions are made by those who do not understand the implications of the detail in front of them. According to him, good managers – albeit in short supply – are capable of compensating for a lack of detailed knowledge in adding value to a range of businesses. While clarity and cohesion of purpose on the part of all are a key ingredient of success, he claims that they are only marginally easier to achieve in a single-focus business. Moreover, conglomerates are much more likely to be dispassionate about their objectives and therefore less likely to pursue the wrong route. Martin argues that it is not a particular change strategy but, rather, the fact of change itself that releases the energy to revitalize a business: 'Focus is not inevitably better than diversity, whatever the conventional wisdom may hold. But change is always better than stagnation.'

LOOKING INTO A RENAISSANCE ORGANIZATION

If it were possible to look inside an organization synthesized from all the components of a Renaissance Organization, what would be seen? Here, it might be useful, as a reference point for understanding the different components, to draw a vision of what an organization that can create and sustain a high-energy relationship with its environment might look like.

A Renaissance Organization will have a dynamic integrated system designed for learning and growth. It will be made up of mobile self-sufficient individuals, who bring both technical competence and a high level of interpersonal skills to the teams in which they work. These teams will include both functional and 'work process' teams, focused on many aspects of the development and delivery of a particular product or service, or on meeting the needs of a particular market niche or locality.

They will be very dynamic and fluid, sometimes self-forming, to meet particular needs in the environment. People will be able to join some teams on a voluntary basis, reflecting the extent to which individuals create their own roles. If a team is not a profit centres in itself, it will be one step from being one, so that feedback from its impact on the business is easily available.

Control will, for the most part, reside with the teams, who will be able to take decisions on a wide range of issues. Co-ordination and strategic direction will be maintained through a number of means, but particularly through the establishment of a comprehensive management information system. Through this, outputs and activities can be measured, and balance between local response and corporate goals created. This reporting system will also underpin the risk management system, which will become increasingly important as organizations are faced with greater uncertainty.

Innovation and the creation of positive differences between the organization and its competitors will be emphasized through specific structures and reward systems, and every employee will recognize these factors as key in the organizational climate. In such a potentially fast-changing environment, leadership will be a collective responsibility, not just an individual role, and networking will be a key skill. This will be further emphasized by an emerging feature of the membership of these organizations: the increasing extension beyond the formal boundaries of full-time employment to include other individuals and other organizations.

Is this all a recipe for chaos? Or an impossible structure? On the contrary, these are all reflections of how different organizations are now trying to cope with the consequences of operating in a complex world.

Having said that there is no ideal structure, it is possible to identify certain components and guidelines that will promote the development of energetic, organizations. These components can be divided into elements – the building blocks or sub-systems required to achieve high levels of flexibility and innovation, and connections. (Note that elements are not the same as structure ie they do not refer to particular functions or parts of the business but the ways that these are assembled to create or save energy.) These elements represent the way an organization links itself together, through a network of relationships, in order that co-ordination and learning may occur for the good of the whole. The elements of a Renaissance Organization can be broadly sub-divided into those that create energy and those that save energy. Put another way, the former are about creating the best possible relationship with the market-place through positioning and local adaptivity, while the latter are about creating the internal efficiencies and ways of working that will enable the organization to deliver its strategy efficiently.

DRAWING ENERGY FROM THE MARKET-PLACE

The design elements for high-energy gain from the market-place are of two different types:

- Operating arrangements that recognize the need for strategic goals delivered through local adaptivity based upon innovation and autonomous decision-making;
- Structures and processes to encourage and capture high-energy strategic positioning through diversity and innovation.

These two broad strands constitute what might be termed a 'complex response'. In trying to align with the market-place, an organization has to both create an overall high-energy strategic position, and respond to local differences. It needs to 'think globally and act locally', as the larger corporations like to say. The necessary structure for a complex response involves integrated differences. It allows for diversity in what different parts of the organization do, and how, and encourages local autonomy, innovation and decision-making. A complex response allows different parts of the organization to be curious, and to experiment within the framework of an overall vision. Nohria and Ghoshal,[2] in their study of multi-national corporations, found that 'overall subsidiary performance is positively correlated with a high degree of internal differentiation, in the same way that differentiation is required for enhancing innovation'. (See also Connections, below.) This experimentation can have both strategic and local benefits. However, for some organizations, saying 'it's OK to be different, to discover your own way of delivering the strategy' can be a big step. Other organizations have been doing it for years. The comfort for such organizations will come through their growing confidence in the integrating processes, which should prevent this experimentation from becoming counter-productive.

CONNECTIONS: SEEKING DIVERSITY AND INTEGRATION[3]

Peter Marsh has compared two companies, one British and one German, in the *Financial Times.* They are both technology leaders, operating globally, and seek diversity, in order to increase their scope outside of their core areas. They are, however, following quite different routes, according to Marsh. Colt, a British company with a turnover of £110 million, specializes in ventilation and related equipment. To extend its offer, its approach is to 'graft on new thinking from the outside'. In pursuit of this, it has added ideas and initiatives through five joint ventures or acquisitions. These moves have taken it into areas of operation, including noise control and solar energy, that are far from their traditional offer.

Seidenader is a Munich-based manufacturer, principally of image analysis systems for checking quality in the pharmaceutical industry. Innovation is being sought, not through external alliances, but by splitting the company in two. Virtually all the company's DM 20m sales come from the pharmaceutical industry and the challenge is to 'spin out' some of its image analysis ideas for use in other sectors. To do this, the company has split itself into two divisions, one to concentrate on traditional markets, the other on new opportunities.

Interestingly, the different routes to delivering innovation have different requirements in terms of the balance to be achieved between integration and diversity. For Colt, the emphasis must be on finding ways to integrate these new alliances with existing management structures and products. Their solution has been to involve over one-quarter of the 1,000-plus staff with the new technologies and ideas that have been brought in. The challenge for Seidenader is almost the opposite – to create sufficient difference between traditional activities to allow it to innovate and experiment in new markets. Therefore, although the company will remain integrated via its common technology, the new division will have a distinct management identity and a joint headquarters in Munich and Pennsylvania. 'To be free to act – in the new division – we have to get away from out pharmaceutical bias,' says Nik Siedenader, who is the great-grandson of the founder, and now runs the company.

LOCAL ADAPTIVITY

It is an assumption of Renaissance Organizations that both local adaptivity and realizing the strategic potential of market positioning will be built from the contribution of all individuals within an organization, not from some specialist role. This will occur through the encouragement of innovation at every level. Given this argument, local adaptivity is also a prerequisite for ongoing and sustainable successful innovation at a strategic level; it captures vital information, generates alternatives, tests ideas, experiments, and challenges head-office or strategic assumptions. Developing the latter will therefore be more than enhanced by establishing the former.

Innovation

Before looking at either of these, it is worth considering the issue of innovation overall. Essentially, what are the conditions that will allow innovation to flourish and become evident in all aspects of an organization's activity? In the article from which the BMW example below is drawn, Michel Syrett and Jean Lammimam identified three characteristics that will allow an organization to promote innovation, both strategically and locally, as follows:

- serendipity;
- individual recognition;
- tolerating the unorthodox.

Serendipity – using chance and coincidence to create meetings between the right people and the right ideas – seems vital to the fostering of innovation. A study by Massachusetts Institute of Technology found that eight out of ten ideas that have ultimately led to 'breakthrough' products or devices have come from chance encounters, casual conversations, or reflection away from the workplace. It seems that the creative juices flow more easily in these situations than in the formal setting of a meeting or focused activity. An important part of these interchanges seems to be that they occur on an individual and personal basis, are usually face to face – based upon a person's individuality, not upon his or her specific role – and take place where non-verbal as well as verbal communication can occur.

Recognizing individual contribution is also an essential part of promoting innovation. Many organizations now run suggestion schemes in which ideas are financially rewarded. I would argue that even more could be gained if individuals were also to be involved in the process by which a particular idea or suggestion is realized.

The third characteristic of an innovative organization is a tolerance for the unorthodox and for dissent. It shows a willingness to entertain and treat seriously ideas that challenge the current perspectives. This reflects the notion of developing challenge and conformity that was discussed earlier.

CONNECTIONS: SERENDIPITY AT BMW[4]

BMW, in developing a new R&D facility, has gone out of its way to increase serendipity. All functions contributing to a new model are physically located together. They worked out which members of staff within this physical location needed to communicate most frequently, and designed the necessary proximity into the office layout. Thus, development design departments are located directly adjacent to their related production planning departments and all design offices are located on the same floors as their model workshop, 'to ensure that staff from each communicate with each other by the shortest possible route'.

Developing local adaptivity

Faced with the need to maintain the best possible energy-gain relationship with the market, Renaissance Organizations need to take local action. 'Local' can mean either a geographical location or a particular part of the business, for example, the front line, that part of the business that is closest to a particular group of stakeholders.

Local adaptivity makes a number of contributions to the energy balance of an equation by taking action close to customers and other stakeholders. It allows for an organization to respond better to the diversity of its stakeholders' needs, and for efficient decision-making and problem-solving, and it keeps the organization as a whole in much closer contact with the realities of the market-place, maximizing its responsiveness to risks and opportunities.

To enable this to happen, the front line of an organization cannot sit about waiting to be told what to do by those further removed from the actual problem or challenge. In many organizations, the front line are forced to sit amazed, or with growing disillusionment, as they see no action being taken and energy being wasted over issues they believe they could quickly resolve. Renaissance Organizations do more than simply give permission for local decision-making; it becomes an absolute requirement.

Local decision-making works in several ways. Greater involvement of staff in innovation, decision-making, and so on, allows individuals to find ways in which they can, and want to, contribute more of their skills, experience and energy. They are also in a position to be the ears and eyes of an organization, helping it identify anything that requires a response at a whole organizational level. This involvement fosters better alignment to customer needs. It creates the conditions for much better customer relationships, in which organizations can move from a goal of customer satisfaction to one of loyalty and involvement. Local autonomy also releases senior management from providing day-to-day direction. This gives them time to evaluate the information they get from the front line and elsewhere to maintain the organization's strategic position, to foster the cross-business sharing of insights and innovations, and to allocate appropriate resources.

Simply, unless there is a good reason to act otherwise, it would be much better for an organization, once it has established goals and performance expectations for a particular part of the business, to let those responsible get on with it. They have the understanding and insight to define the ways in which an organization should pursue its goals, in the light of local realities. They are also in the best position to take decisions concerning the most appropriate ways of creating the structures and processes that would meet both local circumstances and strategic goals.

The challenge here is that organizations need to allow for self-organization at a local level and, indeed, to welcome it. The degree to which this can occur will be determined by many factors, including the technological systems that are in place, the nature of the market, and so on. Organizations could adopt a 'principle of self-determinism', in which serious justifications for not allowing, rather than allowing, should be the basis for limiting authority in these matters. One of the features of seeing organizations as systems is that any system, including a social system, is intrinsically self-organizing. Therefore, given that self-organization will happen anyway, it makes much more sense to acknowledge and resource it, rather than discourage it. The examples of the French company and the flour mill (see below) suggest that this approach warrants serious consideration.

As long as the means for self-organization can be realized, it will be necessary to focus on the formal expectations of the people who work on the front line of the business. Often, these expectations, in turn, will depend upon an individual's scope to create and develop the role that he or she is expected to fulfil. The degree to which an individual is able to innovate his or her role will be a key factor in determining local and organizational responsiveness, as well as the individual's capacity for adaptive innovation and decision-making.

CONNECTIONS: LOCAL ADAPTIVE INNOVATION AND DECISION-MAKING[5]

In the early 1990s, Rank Hovis was ready to close its flour mill in Selby, North Yorkshire. It had the highest operating costs and lowest productivity of any of the company's 11 mills. Rather than face redundancy, the local workforce put together a plan that has had remarkable results. Customer complaints have been reduced by 50 per cent, the number of accidents has fallen by 46 per cent, and flour production has increased dramatically. In 1990, production of flour ran at 100 hours a week. By 1995, production was 163 hours a week. Hours lost to maintenance are now minimal.

There were several key elements to this plan:

- matrixing, in which everyone is capable of performing two or more roles;
- job titles being retained only for the benefit of head-office staff; and
- information being accessible to everyone, and all meetings being open.

In the past, employees were not aware of how their performance was being measured. They now understand in detail such factors as unit cost, and the influence each of them can have upon them. Job swaps are encouraged and flexibility is emphasized everywhere. These changes were not driven by head office, but by local innovation and decision-making.

A potential structural blockage to self-organization is the role of the company policemen, otherwise called 'managers'. Whatever the manager's role in a new organization, it can no longer be principally one of control. Organizations need to remove structures of control where they are no longer appropriate. The test is to imagine that such structures do not exist at all, and to examine very carefully why they should be re-imposed. When the structures have been removed, it is also important to check that old behaviours and processes do not linger.

Many organizations reduced levels of management in the 1980s and 1990s, but their main reason for doing this was essentially cost control. Little effort was made to develop or explain new ways of working, and there was no real focus on creating better-quality internal processes and higher-value transactions. The result was that some key processes became more inefficient, although there was a reduction in cost in other areas. However, there was also a dramatic increase in work demands, and we may just be beginning to see the backlash.

The relationship of employee with stakeholders, and with the organization itself, is traditionally defined by a job description. It is rare for such a document to emphasize curiosity or experimentation. Areas of decision-making and responsibility are ruled out as much as they are ruled in. Perhaps organizations should consider getting rid of formal job descriptions altogether – in any case, many are kept in a bottom drawer and rarely referred to, reflecting their distance from the real demands made upon front-line staff. If job descriptions are kept as part of the formal definition of an organization's structure, then they should at least be expressed in a way that emphasizes local innovation and decision-making. Moreover, the processes by which an individual's performance is monitored and rewarded should also reflect these needs.

CONNECTIONS: SELF-DETERMINATION[6]

One of the most interesting speakers at an Anglo-French Colloquium in Paris in 1996 was a French managing director called Henri Lachmann. He certainly seemed to have allowed for a bottom-up strategy in the way organizations could be designed and run. He also placed this firmly in the context of an organization interacting with its environment, insisting that organizations cannot grow in a sick environment.

Within Lachmann's own company, things seemed to be built up from a local level. Forms of organization, he said, should be negotiated at a local level. To encourage this flexibility, he argued that it was important to disconnect the total wage bill from the total number of employees. He was clearly unimpressed with headcount as a management tool, and regarded its predominance as another example of the rigidity that he felt all organizations must perpetually fight.

Lachmann is convinced that we can be much more innovative and creative about how we develop more flexible organizations. In one example, he outlined an organization that had existed on high levels of overtime, with the usual productivity inefficiencies that sustained levels of overtime can produce. Negotiations at local level led to the annualization of hours, which led to costs savings, increased productivity and the creation of 75 new jobs. Importantly, this arrangement was worked out in the light of local circumstances and what was important both to the organization and its employees.

According to Lachmann, there is no general solution to how an organization should design and run itself. Optimally, it will be the result of an equation between organizational goals and local circumstances.

Lastly, it is important to state that creating local autonomy through self-determinism does not automatically lead to innovation and adaptivity.

Rather, this will be guaranteed by the connecting processes that are put in place, especially the connection through climate and goals. However, building an organization on the basis of self-determinism and the contribution of every individual will be a pre-requisite if enabling levels of innovation and adaptivity are to take place.

Energy gain through strategic positioning

A strategic position is the second of the energy-generating elements of a Renaissance Organization. Positioning can be defined as the relationship that an organization has with the market. Ideally, it should be one through which the least energy is expended for the most gain. The goal is differentiation, making the product or service offered look positively different to that of the competitors.

There are two broad aspects to achieving this:

- creating an innovative offer that competitors will have difficulty copying; and
- given the unpredictability in which organizations operate, experimenting with more than one approach and position.

Simply put, it is a good idea to bet on more than one winner and, wherever possible, avoid 'me too' strategies that leave the organization looking too much like its competitors. Structures that encourage innovation and diversity should be developed.

Experimenting with more than one approach and position is one way of strategically betting on the unknowable. In an unpredictable world, the real wins may occur in areas that neither an organization nor its competitors can foresee. To an extent, diversity is a way of managing risk. It recognizes that there is no one best way, and seeks to benefit from the strategic opportunities that diversity allows. There will be an added advantage of seeing the organization as a complex structure, which can experiment at a limited or local level with a number of different innovations before attempting an organization-wide approach. Another benefit is the much earlier diagnosis of problems, and the acquisition of real rather than hypothetical data for evaluation. This is an approach that adds value to the concept of local adaptivity.

Given the complexity of the market, having more than one potential strategic response will be an advantage; the winners will be those who have the shortest distance to travel to capture an emerging strategic position, and who find they have a head start within their complex response. For example, a company might be doing well with a service or product within a particular market niche, but at the same time it will be using its understanding of its customers to anticipate new and different products and services. It is then better prepared for when the original offer begins to lose its attractiveness, or is suddenly made obsolete by the actions of a competitor.

On the surface, keeping options open in this way may seem to be a waste of energy, but organizations do need this variety and need to avoid playing too safe. Ian Stewart,[7] writing of a need for research into mathematics that is developed for more than immediate pay-off, has written that

> *the pursuance of safe research will impoverish us all. The really important breakthroughs are always unpredictable. It is their very unpredictability that makes them important: they change our world in ways we didn't see coming.*

What is true of the variety of mathematics is also true of the variety of strategic response. Organizations take a risk when they put all their medium-term eggs in one, potentially short-term basket.

Undoubtedly, the result is untidy and can have inefficiencies, but positioning an organization within volatile market-places is bound to require experimentation. This is particularly relevant in some markets, such as financial services, where the life span of certain products can be measured in weeks, and organizations do not have the time for lengthy market research and product testing. To an extent, this 'messiness' can be counterbalanced by the networking and simple structures recommended below.

CONNECTIONS: CONNECTING INNOVATION

The market-place is full of examples of innovations that were developed for one thing, but were more successful in a different application, or were discovered accidentally in the pursuit of something else. Such innovations are not uncommon in the pharmaceutical industry, and other accidents that have created new markets have included the ubiquitous post-it notes, and blue-tac. Similarly, organizations have found themselves with a market opportunity caused by an unforeseen change in fashion. Furthermore, particular structures, or 'configurations of activities', may suddenly confer market advantage.

There is obviously a limit to diversity, but its contribution to the 'possibilities' of an organization should not be ignored.

Of course, strategic positioning through innovation has to mean more than simply rolling the dice on a few opportunities. Processes and structures that promote and capture it need to be put in place. In Renaissance Organizations, this will require considerable involvement, not from some specialized strategic department, but from the whole of the business, particularly those in the front line, closest to the customer and other stakeholders.

The demand for innovation occurs at both local and strategic levels. What is important is that the two are connected in some way. Much of the data highlighting the fact that radical innovation at a strategic level is called for will arise from the front line. People here may discover that it is becoming increasingly difficult through local innovation and decision-making to maintain high-value energy relationships, and may be seeking, or already have the radical solution that the whole organization requires.

However, if strategic innovation is going to happen, more than local autonomy will be required. Innovative ideas and relevant information from the front line are unlikely to succeed strategically if there is no means by which their innovations can go forward. This will be the case for the radical innovations implied here. For an individual or local team to contribute at an organizational level, the following have to be in place:

- local structures that encourage creativity and opportunity-spotting; and
- a very clear process in which people believe.

In summary, processes need to be created to

- identify when an opportunity or need for innovation arises;
- capture that need and translate it into a potential response; and
- resource and implement that response.

A co-ordinated response by the organization as a whole will be required. Structurally, the first requirement will therefore be some reference point to which these emerging issues and ideas can be communicated. The front-line staff need to feel there is somewhere to go, where someone will listen to them. Individuals and teams need access to the corporate whole, and the leverage to influence action.

One suggestion could be a regular innovation-needs forum, open to all, but compulsorily attended by those members of the organization's top team who are seen to have power and influence. Local information and ideas could be mixed with information gleaned from other sources, and the forum could also be a vehicle through which creativity and new ideas could be given sufficient credibility to be properly evaluated. The innovation forum would need be resourced, both in terms of full-time (but temporary) staff and part-time volunteers. This executive would be responsible for further evaluation and for driving the best response, and, if changes are required, establishing the most appropriate

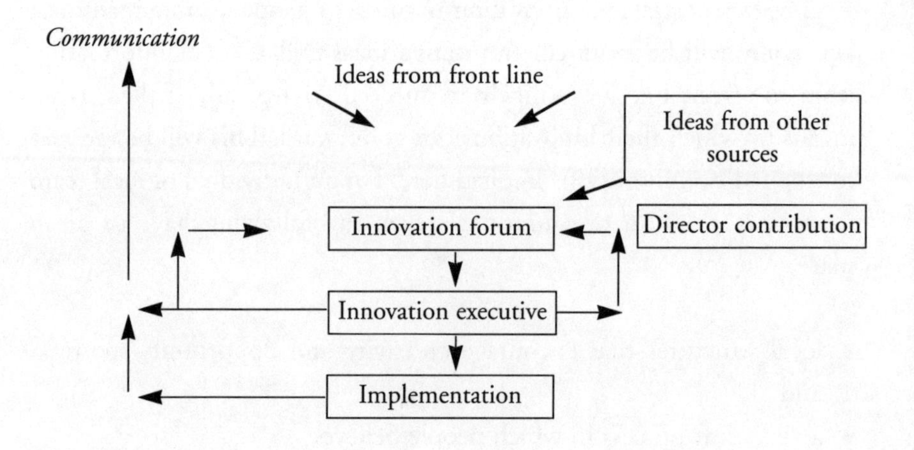

Fig. 6.1 The process of an innovation-needs forum

implementation strategy. A fundamental feature of all aspects of this approach would be that it would need to be cross-functional, enabling it to take a multi-perspective view of the challenges that are faced. The process is summarized in Fig. 6.1.

One advantage of an innovation-needs forum is that all ideas can be much better tested for implementation problems before they are put into practice. Creating a structure like this gives visible recognition to the importance of innovation, and the connectedness of strategy with operating practice, and could do much to highlight issues that may otherwise remain hidden. In an essentially open and cross-functional forum, all perspectives on a problem or a potential solution can be aired. In addition, implementation is potentially enhanced by a greater awareness and understanding of the parts that have to be played.

It is worth noting that, whereas quality circles and focus groups targeted at efficiency issues have been established in many organizations, there is relatively little evidence of time and investment being allocated at the same level to innovation. There has been a variety of low-level suggestions schemes, but these are rarely adequate, and are often used as an excuse for not developing proper local adaptive innovation. Despite this neglect, innovation is fundamental to energy gain; as discussed in

Chapter 7, energy efficiency has received much more attention from the point of view of establishing robust processes.

CONNECTIONS: COMPETING THROUGH INNOVATION[8]

Broderbund Software Inc. is a highly successful pioneer in the PC-based education/entertainment software market. The company's senior vice president, Mr Wilker, has identified the following key ingredients of the successful management of creativity:

- fostering good communication;
- trusting your people;
- realizing the entire organization is creative and good ideas can come from anywhere;
- making sure there is well-conceived documentation for every project;
- checking milestones along the way; evaluating prototypes, keeping projects flowing;
- having the ability to champion projects but also to kill projects, if the economics or markets demands it;
- avoiding divisive practices; and
- knowing when and how to shake up stalled projects.

He also confirms that the motivation for creativity is not driven by financial reward. Most of his creative people have done the same work at some point in their life for free.

Provocations

Does the company have the following?

- Wherever possible a diversity of approaches to the market-place?
- A forum, with top-management support, to capture and implement innovation at all levels?
- Ways for continuous innovation to be measured and reported on and built into the policies and procedures of the organization?
- Local autonomy on innovation, decision-making and even structure and processes?
- An understood basis upon which the front line of the organization is not allowed to make decisions?

References

1. Martin, P (1997) The case for conglomerates, the *Financial Times*, 20 March.
2. Nohria, N and Ghoshal, S (1997) *The Differentiated Network*, Jossey Bass, California.
3. Marsh, P (1997) Same aims, different strategies, the *Financial Times*, 23 December.
4. Syrett, M and Lammimam, J (April 1997) The art of conjuring ideas, *Director*, London.
5. Merrick, N (May 1995) Making the best of the daily grind, *People Management*, IPD, London.
6. Lachmann, H (November 1996) Changes in workplace organization, Anglo-French colloquium, *The Changing World of Work*, Fondation Singer-Polignac, Paris. Organized by the British Council.
7. Stewart, I (1995) *Nature's Numbers: Discovering order and pattern in the universe*, Phoenix, London.
8. Rifkin, G (1998) Competing through innovation: the case of Broderbund, *Strategy and Business*, New York. Second quarter.

CHAPTER 7

THE DYNAMIC, FLEXIBLE AND RESPONSIVE ORGANIZATION

BUILDING BLOCKS

THE PARADOX of responding to a complex environment is that, if the response is to be efficient, it needs to be built of simple elements. There are two reasons for this. First, complicated arrangements absorb more energy in themselves than simple ones. (For example, a very bureaucratic department will create lots of paperwork and routines, and will take more time and effort to do its tasks than one that is more streamlined and empowered.)

Secondly, re-arranging organizations to keep pace with rates of change in the market-place will take energy; the more fixed and formalized an organization, the more energy will be required to change it. The ideal is to have flexible arrangements that can be assembled and disassembled in response to market need. Designing for energy efficiency will therefore require simple structures that are both flexible and responsive.

SIMPLE, ENERGY-EFFICIENT STRUCTURES

Organizational structures are built up of frameworks of relationships, connected by processes that enable transactions to occur. Assuming that energy will be lost cumulatively at each transaction, more energy will be lost in an organization whenever another link is added, in the form of relationships or processes. The most efficient organization, from a transactional point of view, is probably a one-person outfit, in which sales, personnel, production and distribution are the same. As that must be somewhat close to overload, we could probably add one more point, as in Fig. 7.1.

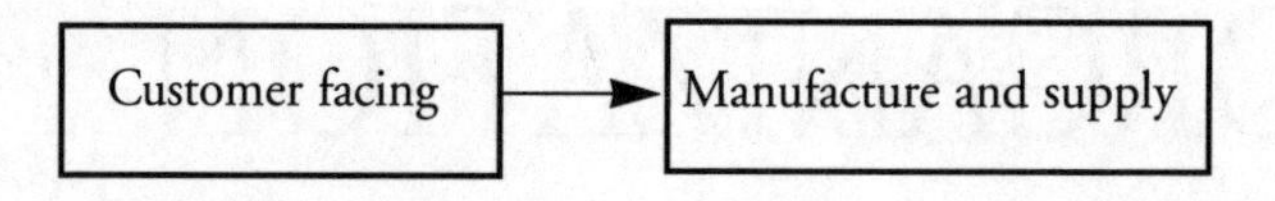

Fig. 7.1 One organizational configuration

Is this impossible? No. It is almost exactly the organizational configuration that Motorola has established for its world-class production of pagers. One person receives the enquiry, makes the sale, takes the specification, raises the invoice and enters all other relevant data. A second person manufactures and arranges dispatch. The pager is in production within eighteen minutes and delivered within twenty-four hours.

Every time a relationship is added to a simple configuration, there is a potential gain in added value for the customer, with a certain loss of energy within the organizational system. If the addition of extra relationships within the system is not intended to add value to the customer, why add it? (Fig. 7.2.) It is too easy, as the next three figures show, to add a complicated superstructure of energy-absorbing transactions to a simple arrangement.

Fig. 7.2 One organizational configuration

Each activity in what is known as the supply chain should contribute to the effectiveness and efficiency of the total process. The supply chain is the sequence of activities that must occur for a customer's needs to be met. According to Michael Porter, each step should be analysed in terms of the way it can add value – create wealth or reduce costs – in terms of the overall process.

Of course, other relationships are traditionally added. In the interests of control, co-ordination and planning, layers of supervision and management are included, and, in order to maintain each of these activities, various support functions are put in place (Fig. 7.3).

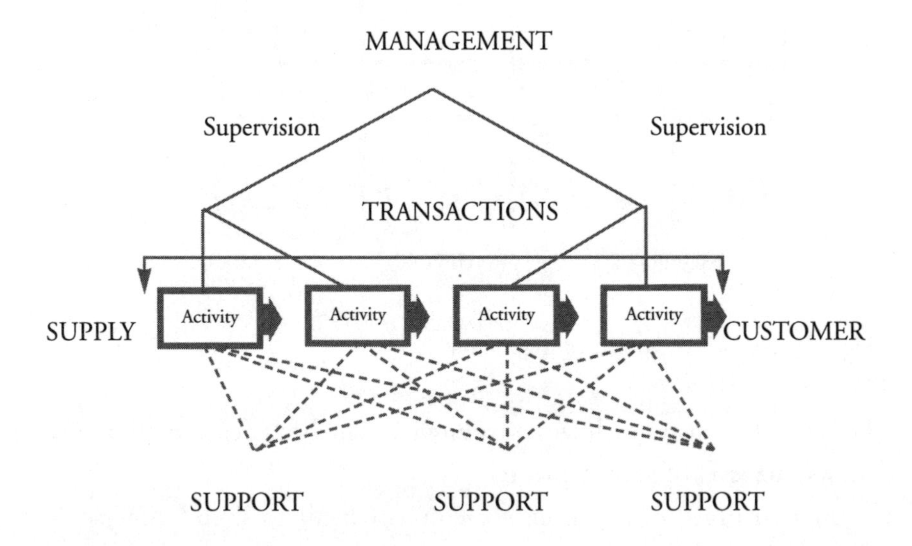

Fig. 7.3 One organizational configuration

Each of the transactions in Fig. 7.3 represents a definite energy loss to be set against a potential energy gain. Traditionally, the primary unit of structure in the design of organizations was not the activity, but the function, such as production, marketing, finance, HR, and so on. In terms of the technology available at the time, and the rate of change within the market-place, these were potentially energy-efficient solutions. However, the effectiveness of these functions was not measured in terms of the value they added to the supply chain and, consequently, energy-absorbing empires incrementally built up. Furthermore, as each activity was broken down into the responsibility of different functions, co-ordination of the activities as a total process became complicated and inefficient. (Fig. 7.4.)

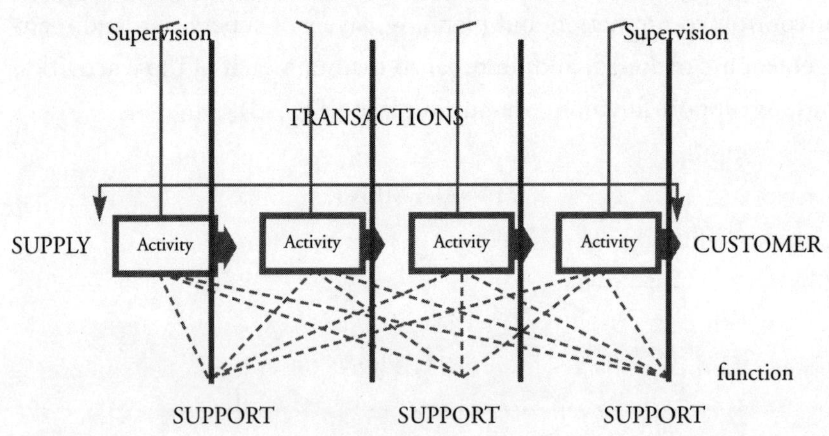

Fig. 7.4 One organizational configuration

Fig. 7.4 demonstrates how convoluted it can become, and this only shows one level of management!

So, over time, organizations – even many medium-sized businesses – have built up huge energy-absorbing structures. However, conditions have changed, particularly the potential for technological innovation, and organizations do not have to be built like this. Why not assume that this level of co-ordination and support is not required? That those involved in the different activities that make up the supply chain can manage the process themselves, and that they will ask for the support needed when they see it will improve the energy they have to maintain this process? Let us imagine for a while how co-ordination of all activities might occur and concentrate on how support might be invoked and delivered. (Co-ordination and control through connectedness will be dealt with in Chapter 8.) On this basis, the following question should be asked of every activity: does it add or save energy for the essential process of transactions by which an organization maintains itself in the market-place? The trick is to discover ways in which all activities can be related to the goals and results of an organization. For example, training is no longer a general activity, but targeted at the needs of particular activities and measured by its impact upon them.

Arguments such as these are often concerned with the extent to which different activities can be said to 'add value'. At one level, value and energy can be treated as almost synonymous, but, if value is narrowly defined in terms of cash or as a short-term financial equation, it is not always appropriate as a way of measuring the contribution of certain activities. It may, for instance, result in the curtailing of activities that have medium-term value or represent a reasonable innovative risk. There is also a pressure to discover financial ways of describing the value activities, which cannot be so easily described; the risk is that they are distorted and their impact is lessened. For example, reducing the impact of, say, an exceptionally well-received PR initiative, to mere financial statistics, misses the essence of the initiative's total benefit to the organization.

Finally, measuring value in short-term, financial considerations, focuses too much on one perspective of organizations – a mechanistic perspective – and does not capture the human side of the energy equation, which relates to such issues as motivation and commitment.

So, how is it possible to measure the energy value of an activity? It rather depends upon the activity. Table 7.1 suggests a number of ways of measuring energy, often linked to performance, but begs the question of how to choose the best ones. Perhaps it is possible to turn the argument on its head. Those responsible for the core operational processes should decide what adds value and energy to them, and decide on suitable measures to make sure they get what they want. This should be done on the basis of the fact that these measures relate to activities that have an impact on their goals and output requirements. This is the simplicity of the energy paradigm: it allows links to be made between different sorts of measures without the need to become bogged down in a hunt for a single sort of dimension to tie everything together. (This is not to remove the need for financial monitoring but to emphasize that other measures are needed as well.)

Table 7.1 Measures of energy

improved team climate;
improvements in productivity;
reduction in error rates;
greater numbers of innovations;
staff morale;
employee flexibility;
improved decision-making;
customer satisfaction ratings;
job satisfaction (inc. Apter Work Impact System).

These arguments are, of course, closely related to those put forward by proponents of business process re-engineering (BPR). BPR seeks to analyse the relationship between customer and supply. The relationship is regarded not from where it is, but from where it should be, in terms of the most efficient, effective and value-adding way of approaching it. Actions are then taken to bridge the gap between current position and desired position. In Renaissance terms, this will be about connectedness to maximize the value of the transaction.

The problem is not in the approach but, rather, in the implementation. At its crudest, process re-engineering takes an extremely instrumental/mechanistic view of organizations. People within organizations are therefore regarded not only as extremely rational, but it is also assumed that they will make their rational decisions on the basis of what is best for the company, although it may not be best for them. The problem with this approach is that it only recognizes energy transactions at a simplistic, instrumental level. This can result in important underlying issues not being recognized. There is a danger of a fixation on one 'mechanistic' perspective of the reality of organizations. The result of this is that the tell-tale signs of problems and issues affecting the successful implementation of more efficient structures are not recognized.

The energy value of a relationship must be expressed in more than immediate (usually financial) terms. An organization needs to take a much more integrated picture before changes can be made, and understand the very real pay-offs that will be involved. Energy is blocked and wasted in many ways. Even the simple transaction described above will be affected by various issues:

- how the two parties get on;
- whether there is clear demarcation of responsibilities and activities; or
- when there are status issues involved.

Designing simple structures that are energy-efficient will therefore require knowledge and skills that are based, not just upon a logical analysis of work processes, but also on the nature and behaviour of people, both individually and in groups. Individuals come to the fore again!

RESPONSIVENESS AND FLEXIBILITY

Responsiveness enables organizations to adapt quickly and consolidate their advantages at a local and strategic level. Key to this will be an organization's ability to mobilize its resources, particularly its people, around a new challenge. (It will also depend upon the availability of sufficient energy, in terms of money, people, information and so on, to drive the change.) Developing responsiveness will require the kind of individual behaviours discussed in Chapter 4, and will have five discernible characteristics:

1. energy focus;
2. boundary-busting flexibility;
3. timing and level of resources;
4. maximization of individual talent and experience;
5. support for improvisation.

Characteristic 1 – energy focus

Organizations need to be totally focused on how they use energy. They need to highlight and tackle how and where energy is used inefficiently. Often a fundamental re-appraisal of the way an organization is put together is needed, as current systems and structures are usually a solution to yesterday's problems.

Characteristic 2 – boundary-busting flexibility

Energy can be wasted in the creation of empires, departments and bureaucratic procedures. Responsiveness must not be held back by false boundaries that exist, not to serve customer needs, but to maintain themselves. Organizations need the ability to mobilize the resources needed for the challenges they face; they should not be blocked by false hierarchies, status, 'departmentalization', and so on. Market needs ignore the subtleties of organizational organograms, and traditional line-management approaches, and organizations need to be able to do the same. They will need to work to produce an openness about all aspects of their system, through which boundaries and functional demarcations can be challenged and overcome.

One of the boundaries that might block mobilization is the formal role description; increasingly, Renaissance Organizations need to accept people innovating and designing their own contribution as an acceptable way of building boundary-busting responsiveness. Some organizations have already started to do this, and one example is Gore-Tex, highlighted below.

CONNECTIONS: CREATING YOUR OWN CONTRIBUTION[1]

Gore-Tex, which makes fabric for sports people, designed its organization around a set of principles known collectively as the 'Lattice Organization':

First there were no employees, only associates. Every associate dealt directly, person to person, with every other, as they wanted and needed. Tasks were neither assigned nor assumed. Associates chose the areas in which they would like to contribute and then made personal, public commitments to themselves and others to make them happen. Discipline and feedback came from peers in the group involved in the implementation of tasks.

Founder Bill Gore established that lattice principles work best in organization units of not more than 150 people. Each unit is composed of multiple overlapping lattices of people, who work together or know each other. Liaison roles between lattices and units play a crucial part. Another key requirement is strong leadership, which is requested by others, not imposed.

Characteristic 3 – timing and level of resources

One of the most difficult management tasks for an organization is to resource change to the proper level. Both under-resourcing and over-resourcing waste energy and dull responsiveness. Organizations in which control of resources has become associated with power will suffer as people withhold or hoard those resources in order to gain leverage over others. A key factor in mobilizing resources is timing. It is no use making the resources available for a project or initiative too soon; energy, like cash or capital, should be engaged as much as possible if it is to be used efficiently. Nor should the resources be made available too late, leading to a failure to consolidate an advantage or solution. A key influence on the timing and level of resourcing will be dependent upon the flexibility of the labour resource.

The French company discussed in Chapter 6 used locally decided flexible working practices to improve the supply side of its business. Organizations also need to consider how they react to fluctuations in demand. Different arrangements for workforce flexibility are being explored – indeed, one or two might be said to verge on exploitation – but it is undoubtedly a key part of any company's strategy to find a path that allows it to be both efficient and flexible at the same time. For example, companies in the IT industry have for a long time been using freelance staff; this allows them to gain the latest expertise as and when they need it, without creating huge overheads. In the case of IT, it is balanced by freelancers demanding high recompense for their flexibility. Charles Handy has written about 'portfolio careers', such as selling professional expertise to a few clients with whom a freelancer may have an ongoing relationship. Other working relationships – such as networking (see below) – will continue to be explored over the next few years, until organizations find an employment pattern that really suits their market and their strategy.

CONNECTIONS: FLEXIBILITY – THE ANNUALIZATION OF HOURS

Britain's Best Factory Awards is an annual competition operated by Cranfield University School of Management and *Management Today*. In 1996, the winner was the Van Den Bergh margarine factory in Purfleet.

Among the building blocks of manufacturing excellence identified by Cranfield,[2] the capacity of a factory to adjust volume levels quickly and easily in response to changes in demand is 'fast becoming the most powerful competitive weapon of the early twenty-first century'.

Van Den Bergh introduced a radical change to its employment terms and conditions, based not just upon excellent teamwork, but also an employment system based upon the principle of 'work when there is work there to be done'. This system of annualized hours has been created to allow the company to respond to the annual peaks and troughs in the factory's order book.

Within the system, the 1779 hours that each employee undertakes to work annually varies by 70-80 hours, as does the shift-pattern work-load. The extra time is available for training, planned extra production or meetings. Employees may also be expected work up to another 282 'committed' hours. These are paid for, whether or not they are worked, but they can only be used to cover equipment failures, or particularly high levels of absenteeism. (Actual consumption of these hours averages around 30 per individual.)

Characteristic 4 – maximization of individual talent and experience

Challenges and problems in the market and the wider business environment do not respect organizational boundaries. They are complex, messy and interrelated. Dealing with them will require people who have an intuitive understanding of the complexity of an organization as a system. They will need energy and resilience, intellectual skills, the ability to influence and lead outside of any formal hierarchy, as well as experience, judgement and the capacity to be flexible enough to cope with the many changes that they will face in a highly responsive organization. They must also be willing to commit all this to an organization. These general traits will be sought in the workforce as a whole, not just in the highly rewarded high-fliers.

Organizations will need to have extensive knowledge of the potential of every one of their employees. Performance management approaches need to encourage a much more individualistic contribution, based upon the sort of psychological contracts discussed in Chapter 1.

Characteristic 5 – improvisation

'Improvisation' is a key skill rarely found in a job specification or list of competencies. It goes against the vision of an organization being an entity that is planned and controlled. It might even be seen negatively as an amateurish, rough-and-ready approach. Improvisation as a business value is not this. It is, rather, a willingness to recognize the reality of complexity, and to fashion a result with the time and resources available. In a dynamic market, it is about working out what should be done and assembling the plans and resources to do it, rather than relying on processes and goals that may have worked in the past, but probably no longer apply. In this, it closely supports the need for innovation and builds truly resilient flexibility.

TEAMS AND NETWORKS

What are the design implications of these considerations? Much has been written about the ways organizations might enhance their flexibility. At a workforce level, this has included drives for multi-skilling, different contracts of employment, team-working, and fewer levels of management. At an organizational level, there has been an increasing use of outsourcing, and partnership arrangements.

Teams

The starting point for these arrangements will be a variety of forms of team-working. These will be the basic working unit, in which innovation and decision-making can occur at a local level, as well as the ongoing delivery of strategy. These teams will not necessarily be the formally constituted teams of the past, but much more ad hoc groupings driven by a particular market or other stakeholder's need. They will come into being as a result of this need, will flourish while that need is still to be met, and will fade away as that need diminishes.

Teams, rather than roles, will make up the building blocks of organizations. It is only through teams that an organization will gain the connectedness of skills, experience and perspectives required to enable flow. Peter Drucker[3] has argued that the emergence of 'knowledge workers' results in work that is highly specialized, and depends upon efforts being co-ordinated as part of an organizational team. This is a situation in which 'teams become the work unit rather than the individual'.

These teams will be discussed more fully in the following chapters, but it is worth discussing certain relevant features at this point. Membership of a team will often be assigned, but should it not also be possible to join these teams on a voluntary basis? These potentially self-forming teams will almost certainly be cross-functional; this is because market needs, or any other stakeholder's needs, will rarely fall simply within a particular artificial boundary created by an organization. If the challenge is that meeting these needs requires several perspectives, then the advantage of the team will be in its cross-functionality and its ability to question different assumptions.

There is plenty of evidence to suggest that these sorts of teams are already starting to appear in organizations. Many people find themselves in more than one cross-functional team, which has been brought together to fulfil some long-term or short-term need. To date, these teams have largely been concerned with more efficient methods of operations, and arrangements such as self-managed teams and work groups are quite common on the shop floor. Cross-functional teams, focused on managing a particular product or service offer, are also appearing. These have more managerial responsibility.

Lars Kolind, CEO of Oticon, a Danish hearing-aid manufacturer, set ambitious targets for his organization in the areas of productivity and innovation. To achieve them, he redefined jobs around individuals, and replaced hierarchies with project groups of multi-skilled workers; these were re-configured constantly according to changing work demands. All communications were transformed from formal memos and meetings to informal conversations. Interestingly, e-mail was also discouraged, to make people communicate face to face.[4]

The question for these teams will be, 'Do we have the right level of autonomy to make the decisions we need to make?' Will individuals be able to join the teams that they need to join? And will these teams feel free to innovate to maintain local connectedness? The ability of front-line teams to take management decisions, rather than basically problem-solve process issues, is far from universally accepted. The example in Chapter 6, of the Rank Hovis mill in Selby, may remain a rare exception.

Networks

Creating a flexible workforce involves much more than simply asking individuals to take on more responsibility, or putting them in teams. Thinking and acting outside of boundaries that have been established through the experience and history of an organization represents a major shift in perspective and behaviour. This shift needs to occur both at the level of the team member and at the level of senior management. Generally, the latter group, despite initiating these moves towards greater flexibility, has the least appreciation of what is required. Why? They have never worked in this way themselves – tackling the problems of gaining approval from line management on cross-functional issues. The result can be a failure to appreciate the ways in which such teams and individuals will need to operate, particularly with regard to the autonomy needed for decision-making, the necessary processes, and relationships with other teams and stakeholders.

As discussed, a Renaissance approach will almost undoubtedly involve an emphasis on a high level of networking. If an organization wants to provide the resources innovation and risk management needed to make an energetic response to the market-place, networking provides a level of alignment and across-boundary flexibility that will be critical. It also offers the chance to maximize individual contribution by linking people to market needs rather than to functional millstones.

Broadly, three levels of networking can be established within an organization, and one or more of these can be emphasized in response to a particular set of conditions. Informal networking is the interpersonal activity through which people can develop an understanding of each other and a broader perspective on what is going on. In particular, an understanding of the more hidden aspects of organizational life can be developed, to increase the individual's own personal effectiveness, through a greater understanding of potential blockages and challenges. In this way, when a rapid response has to be made, or a team or group quickly formed, individuals will have a much better grasp of the reality of the issues they face. It is a key part of aligning the people in the organization with the market-place.

A more structured network occurs when the collaboration required by individuals is more formally recognized. This often takes the form of matrix management, whereby an individual may have a functional responsibility, and will also be answerable to a project group or team that is looking cross-functionally at a particular challenge.

Matrix management offers a tempting route to flexible resourcing of new initiatives and cross-functional challenges. However, a mind shift must take place if it is to operate successfully. People need to see how they fit into their organization in new ways, and working this out will be a considerable challenge. All sorts of issues, to do with interpersonal relationships, power bases, and the way issues are resolved between different groups, lie just beneath the rational surface of this way of working. In particular, functional line management can find these moves quite frightening, as they see their influence over their 'subordinates' diminish. Matrix management represents the erosion of the traditional functional power bases of an organization. Great care needs to be taken to deal with the expectations of the line managers. They need to be helped to develop a new conception of their role, so that they continue to be willing to devote considerable energy to the organization.

At its worst, matrix management can be a fudge between the historical and traditional structures of hierarchical functional management and the emerging needs for a true network structure. For many organizations, there needs to be a sequence of development between each of the levels of networking. In other words, efforts made to encourage informal networking may well enhance the future introduction of matrix management as a preparation for a true network structure.

Some organizations have attempted a much more complete form of network structure. In these cases, people have moved away from functional role definitions all together, and over to a more general portfolio of skills. The example of Gore-Tex illustrates this. While such structures potentially offer incredible levels of flexibility, as people cluster around a challenge, project or issues, creating a unique blend of skills and experience, they also require sophisticated interpersonal and self-management behaviours. In most cases, these will need to be developed. They will also require intense levels of communication. A workforce capable of this level of sophistication will be very difficult to build. It will require what amounts to cultural transformation for many organizations, and a revolutionary change in the expectations of individual contribution and performance.

External networking

So far, we have discussed the potential for networks within organizations. It is now increasingly common for organizations to exist within networks themselves. (It is not uncommon among particularly research-based organizations such as pharmaceutical companies to allow or even encourage networking between individuals of different companies to facilitate learning and innovation.) These can be referred to as strategic partnerships, alliances or joint ventures. There are three broad reasons for establishing such networks, all of which are aimed at reducing energy demands:

- to gain scale without mass – looking bigger in the market-place without increasing fixed costs, overheads, and so on;
- to bring together skill sets or competencies that do not exist within one organization; or
- to manage risk by outsourcing operations or processes that the organization finds difficult to do efficiently to its required level of quality.

All these issues could be dealt with by an organization itself, but they would use more energy, particularly in the short term. (Set against this may well be reduced energy gain in the medium term, for example, through decreased returns, and so on; this trade-off will be a matter of judgement for those responsible.) These structures allow organizations to respond flexibly to market opportunities in very short timescales. There are many examples of the creation of these virtual structures; no doubt they will become an increasing feature of organizational life.

James Quinn,[5] writing of the power of strategic outsourcing of parts of an organization's activities, emphasizes that

> *by selectively relying on outside specialists, companies can lower their capital investment significantly… increasing their capital turnovers to three or more times that of more integrated competitors. Strategic outsourcing provides the buyer with greater stability, especially when purchasing rapidly developing new technologies, fashion goods. It allows the buyer to obtain the full economies of scale and scope of the world's most sophisticated suppliers… such outsourcing also spreads the company's risk for component or subsidiary technology developments among a number of suppliers.*

He notes that both Nike and Apple, in its heyday, are two organizations that successfully managed this.

CONNECTIONS: NETWORK EXAMPLES

Examples of using networks to gain scale without mass would include franchising arrangements and, at a more local level, the formation of loose networks of consultants in order to pitch for larger contracts.

The link between Matra and Renault produced both an innovative product and a new market niche – the Espace people carrier. Renault benefited from Matra's flair for product concepts, design capabilities and manufacturing competence. Renault provided greater levels of experience and resource in marketing, distribution, and service.

James Quinn emphasizes that creating a network of outsourced activities can minimize risk by enabling companies to switch suppliers and take advantage of the latest in developments, including technological developments. One company that has always outsourced significantly is IBM. In 1992, only ten minutes of direct internal assembly was involved in producing an IBM PC. IBM's suppliers continuously change as new suppliers offer higher-quality or lower-cost components.

CONCLUSIONS

This brief examination of different aspects of networking brings us full circle and raises issues again about strategic positioning. If an organization can gain flexibility and energy by outsourcing a variety of its activities, there is a danger that, in using world-class suppliers also available to its competitors, it will lose its ability to differentiate itself in the market-place. Building high-energy Renaissance Organizations will continually involve such decisions – looking at the pay-off between saving energy and gaining it through strategic differentiation and innovation.

The point is not that all organizations should become highly networked structures. However, the solution does exist, and organizations, in creating their high-energy response, will seek to use it wherever it makes energetic sense. The potential solution is enhanced by the opportunity of increasing flexibility provided by IT (see Chapter 8).

Provocations: Renaissance Organization components

Does the company have the following?

- Simple structures, with every additional link having to prove that it adds energy or saves it before it is approved?
- A basic work unit of teams that will be cross-functional and, where possible, self-forming?
- Network structures, both within the organization, and between the organization and others?

References

1. Hastings, C (1993) *The New Organization – Growing the culture of organizational networking*, McGraw-Hill, Maidenhead.
2. New, C (Winter 1997) The building blocks of manufacturing excellence, *Management Focus*, **9**, Cranfield University School of Management.
3. Drucker, P (November 1994) Teams: The age of social transformation, *The Atlantic Monthly*.
4. Syrett, M and Lammimam, J (April 1997) The art of conjuring ideas, *Director*, London.
5. Quinn, J B (1992) *Intelligent Enterprise*, Free Press, New York.

CHAPTER 8

HOLDING THE RENAISSANCE ORGANIZATION TOGETHER: MAKING CONNECTIONS

THIS CHAPTER is about what holds a Renaissance Organization together. It focuses on how organizations can pass responsibility down to the people at the front line, and benefit from the advantages of this, without collapsing into chaos. In particular, it examines the relationships and the processes that would do the following:

- involve everyone, both in what the organization is trying to achieve and the circumstances in which it is trying to achieve it;
- communicate a whole range of important issues up, down and across the organization;
- promote individual and organizational learning and maximize the benefits of innovation;

- relate planned position to actual position;
- identify the opportunities and risks that are faced; and
- gain the necessary information to make a response.

KEEPING IT TOGETHER

It is fine to promote flexibility and responsiveness through local decision-making, autonomy and empowerment, but how does an organization put in place the checks and balances that it needs in order to maintain its coherence and achieve its strategic goals? These checks and balances are essential if the organization is to be more than a loose confederation of small units spinning ever further away from its centre.

The emerging implication of this is that organizations will have to work hard to establish new ways of connecting themselves. They will have to select from a range of tools and techniques, in order to achieve the benefits of their collective resources, and to maintain a coherent sense of direction.

This second point is worth emphasizing. One of the effects of the changes that are creating the need for a high-energy response is a requirement to connect employees much more to the strategy of the organization. Everyone needs to know what they are expected to contribute to achieving the goals of the total business. Local parts of the business need the freedom to respond to local stakeholders' circumstances, to find the best ways of achieving those goals. The question remains: how is it possible to connect local action to strategic direction in a way that maximizes the energy potential of the whole?

From a mechanistic perspective alone, the challenge is significant. What mechanisms should be put in place to ensure that efforts are co-ordinated, and resources are used effectively and efficiently? For example, in giving different parts of the business responsibility for their own recruitment, how is it possible to establish effective, high-quality succession planning across the company? Or, in giving different parts of the business their own control over resource utilization planning, by what means is it possible to prevent local effectiveness turning into corporate inefficiencies? Issues such as these are in themselves manageable, but their complexity is rarely anticipated as organizations change.

However, the problem is wide and deep. In my career as a consultant I have often come up against the difficulties caused by changes, where the issues of operational, personal and communications relationships have not been thought through. Organizations consist of much more than formal, or 'mechanical' linkages; the truth of the complex and informal linkages that make up the real way an organization binds itself should be self-evident. It is this fabric of interwoven links and strands that is broken up by almost any change, yet little time and fewer resources are devoted to replacing it. The result is that the flow of energy is disrupted precisely at the point where it is most needed.

CONNECTIONS: THE HIDDEN LINKS

In more than one organization, I have found that re-engineering led to functional structures being replaced by more matrix-based arrangements. People found that, as well as their functional responsibilities, they were also within teams, focused on responsibilities for one particular product or service line. Several problems presented themselves to these teams, essentially centred around working out how to make these new arrangements work on the ground. No amount of pre-planning could deal with the detail of how, at an individual and interpersonal level, people were expected to work with each other.

To those involved, working life can suddenly seem confusing and unclear, and lacking in structure. One of the reasons for this is that the old way – for all its faults – had been made to work, not through planning and analysis, but through negotiation, convention and interpersonal skills such as influence and networking. These solutions to the inherent difficulties of the past had evolved over time, in more stable conditions; but time and stability are missing in the current scenario.

The interventions that seem to work, and improve people's ability to operate successfully within these new arrangements, are based upon developing the skills and approaches highlighted in this book. Principally, they focus on finding the means of re-connecting individuals and groups back into the organization as a whole, in ways that will promote their effectiveness. Given the current nature of organizations, these interventions relate as much to improving the way people network and negotiate, as to more formal structures and processes.

PROMOTING CONNECTEDNESS

Characterizing the opposing forces at work as a need for strategic direction and local autonomy, it can be argued that connectedness builds a bridge between the two (see Fig. 8.1).

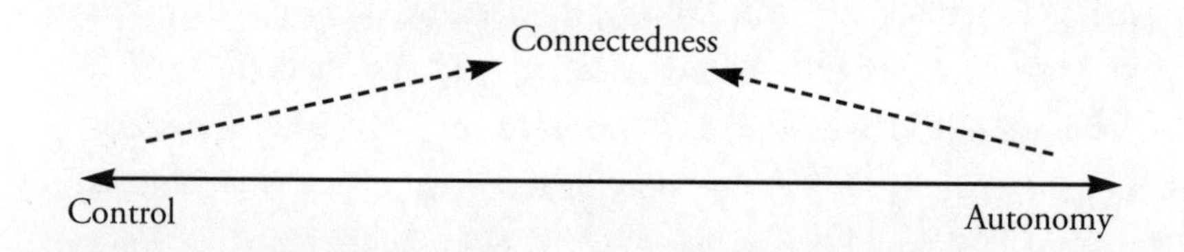

Fig. 8.1 Building bridges

Connectedness is not about control – if control is about command and direction. Although control might have been good enough to manage a compliant workforce, connectedness seeks to join the creativity, energy and desire for autonomy of the individuals and team with the needs of the organization. Therefore, connectedness will need to be the following:

- about hearts as well as minds; and
- a two-way process.

Involving hearts as well as minds is about creating the conditions in which an individual is prepared to commit his or her considerable resources of energy, creativity and wider experience to an organization. In addition, the individual will be prepared to support and promote the success of others within the organization as well as their own. Too often, company culture and, more specifically, performance management systems, reward a very individual sort of effort and rarely acknowledge the contribution made by an individual to the success of others. Connectedness recognizes the interdependence that should exist within all parts of the organization, and deliberately seeks to promote it.

In the end, this connectedness is about allowing energy to flow, not just within the strategically positioned, efficient processes discussed above, but also between them. Management style will be a crucial factor in this, but an organization also has several other levers available that it can pull in order to promote a stronger connectedness. Organizations need to construct a coherent strategy for this connectedness using certain approaches.

ALIGNMENT

The ideal of connectedness and the processes by which it is developed is to create alignment between all the stakeholders' needs within the energy equation. This alignment is the ultimate goal, but it is never achieved because of the paradoxical nature of individuals and organizations. The struggle to build alignment will employ combinations of the connecting processes outlined to influence an organization positively within the following four perspectives of that organization:

- how it is engineered;
- the types of relationships that exist;
- the reconciliation of differing needs through negotiation; and
- creating a positive balance of power.

(See Chapter 11 for a detailed explanation of the impact of these perspectives.)

It would be over-simplistic to assign a particular technique or issue to one particular perspective. For example, it would be wrong to claim that management information systems address purely the engineering/instrumental aspects of organizations and do not have an impact on the organization from other perspectives. They do; in fact, management information systems effectively using the power of technology can radically alter the balance of power within an organization.

In summary, the following ways of establishing connectedness with a goal of producing alignment are available to an organization:

- Connectedness through organizational vision.
- Connectedness through HR processes.
- Connectedness through open management information systems.
- Connectedness through learning and risk management.
- Connectedness through mentorship.
- Connectedness through communication.
- Connectedness and climate.
- Connectedness through ownership.
- Connectedness through networks and negotiation.
- Connectedness by management.

CONNECTEDNESS THROUGH ORGANIZATIONAL VISION

Many of the arguments for a Renaissance approach have emphasized the need for an empowered front line and for local autonomy, particularly in the way individuals, teams and business units operate. This might sound like a call to abandon corporate strategy and goals. Nothing could be further from the truth. In a Renaissance approach, clarity relating to goals and strategy is paramount. These goals will ultimately reflect the need for an organization to add value to its shareholders (literally, or, in not-for-profit organizations, metaphorically), but will also reflect the values of the company and the principles by which it chooses to do business.

An organization's strategic position should reflect the organization's vision of itself. Its vision statement should cover the purpose of the company, its aspirations and its strategy. It can be summarized in the answers to the following three questions:

- What are we? (purpose)
- Where do we want to go? (aspirations)
- How do we want to get there? (strategy)

The answers will represent the vision of the organization and, whatever the level of autonomy or differentiation, they should be the reference point for any decision about change. There is not enough space here to go into all the issues of producing a vision statement for an organization, but it should fundamentally encapsulate the purpose and identity of an organization, so that it has value for anyone responsible for a decision; this really means everyone in the organization. Too many vision statements are bland; they seem to be filled with good intent, but have little connection with reality. Many need to be re-drafted.

A strategic vision should be like a magnet pulling the disparate parts of an organization together, to enable it to work for high-energy flows to become a reality. A key part of the vision should be the extent to which it reflects and requires a drive for strategic innovation and differentiation. All visions should be directed towards the creation of a high-energy environment.

CONNECTIONS: CREATING A VISION STATEMENT

This example is drawn from some work I did in Romania with senior managers from a variety of backgrounds. The work was sponsored by the European Union and looked to develop tools for greater innovation. As part of the work, we looked at the role of vision and strategy as a way of providing focus on those areas in which innovation could make the most useful impact.

Q: *What are we?*
A: A major provider of automotive parts in Eastern Europe.

Q: *Where do we want to get to?*
A: Being recognized as an organization that always meets the highest customer expectations in terms of quality, delivery and customer service.

Q: *How do we want to get there?*
A: (Among other things) by sourcing the best possible partners for manufacture and distribution.

CONNECTEDNESS THROUGH HR PROCESSES

Not surprisingly, HR has a key role to play in developing the connectedness of organizations. Through many of its activities, it can inculcate a value set of shared values and ideas that encourage or discourage connectedness. For example, Procter and Gamble[1] creates teams whose members are drawn from different national organizations in Europe, to co-ordinate regional strategies for different products of the company. By ensuring that general mangers from different subsidiaries head each team, the company has 'deliberately created reciprocal interdependence'. (The level of co-operation the general mangers could expect from the other subsidiaries depends upon how co-operative the general manager or his or her subordinates were with the general managers of other product teams.)

Induction processes also have a role to play in creating connectedness. Matsushita recruits college graduates as managers and develops them together as a large cohort over more than a year. Phillips, by contrast, recruits locally and in small numbers, and there is little central development of managers. The result is that Matsushita managers show a strong commitment to collective values; at Phillips, views are less homogenous and there is a greater willingness to change at local levels.[2] Neither policy is intrinsically 'right'; the important point is that induction does make a difference and that organizations need to take a view of where it places them on the differentiation/integration continuum.

CONNECTEDNESS THROUGH OPEN MANAGEMENT INFORMATION SYSTEMS

It is difficult to see how any organization, except for the very smallest, could operate successfully without an effective management information system. It would be like trying to fly an aircraft through a storm without any instruments.

The impact of information technology allows the head office of an organization to communicate directly with the front line, and vice versa. Essentially, this, in Peter Gibbins' words, 'democratizes' the organization. Organizations can now communicate and shape their destiny through a network, not through a series of management levels in which 'Chinese whispers' will inevitably play a part. Usually, people are able to take corrective action as long as they can see how they are going in relation to some strategic imperative. They can also share in the performance and learning of others. If there is deviation, it is much easier for the head office to intervene and find out why. Intervention is not necessarily about control; indeed, once a feedback system is in place, it should be easier for the head office not to interfere.

Fig. 8.2 summarizes the key facets of a connecting, risk-managing information system. This model allows for the capture of data direct from the front line, which not only can be acted upon locally, but can also be transmitted back to the centre of the organization for learning and risk management. It also allows for the dissemination of the collective wisdom and needs of the organization back out to the front line in terms of strategy and vision. There are two key elements to the model – orientation and feedback loops – which organizations need to consider carefully. It is through these two that the centre of an organization maintains the integration of its parts behind its strategy. The way they are established will therefore be critical.

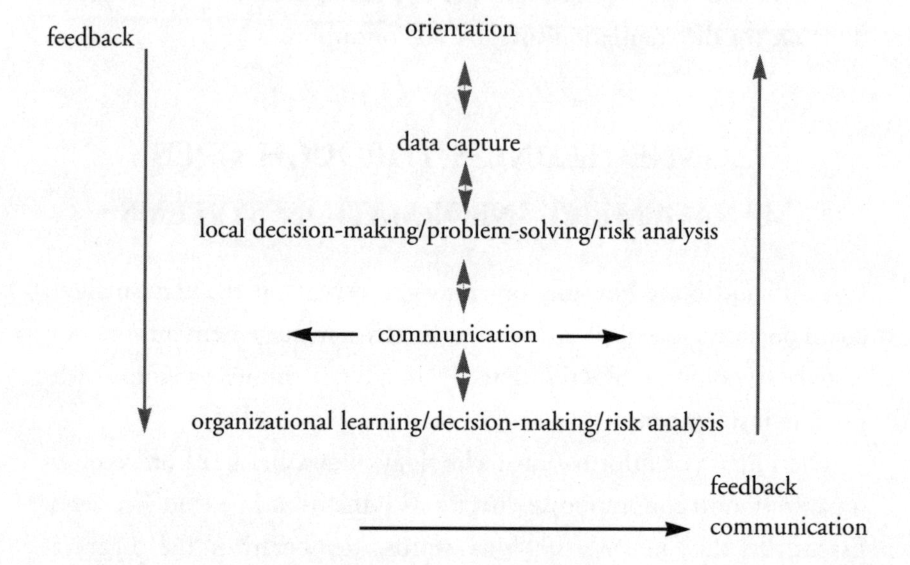

Fig. 8.2 A connecting, risk-managing information system

Orientation

There are some difficulties in setting up a workable response, in terms of structure and process, to the demands this creates for the capture of up-to-date data. One of the intrinsic problems of management information systems is that they provide too much data, resulting in unread or ignored print-outs, reports, and so on. The data remains raw material, which is not given meaning by context or relationship to organizational or individual priorities; in fact, it never actually becomes 'information'.

The answer should be the provision of an orientation or focus, based upon the vision suggested in the model above, which allows relevant data to be captured, and to become information to which a response can be made. However, one of the paradoxes of operating in a complex environment is the need to reduce the amount of data, set against the fact that quite small details outside the focal area could have a dramatic impact.

The demand therefore, in design terms, is to provide the means by which the captured data, which has been turned into meaningful information, remains manageable and capable of response at a local, as well as organizational level. In addition, an organization needs a structure that enables it to spot, either as an opportunity or a threat, the 'wild ball'.

One way to promote this is through a clarity of vision and strategy, which allows the front line to recognize what is relevant and what is not. Another way is to provide – as with structures for innovation – a forum for communicating and highlighting, issues that have more of a basis in gut feel and intuition.

Establishing feedback loops

Measures need to be created and maintained so that each individual knows the impact of his or her actions, or the impact of changes in the market environment, and is able to change his or her own behaviour as a result. Moreover, this information should be quantifiable, so that comparisons can be made and transmissions facilitated. There are cultural reasons for this too – people in organizations are used to responding to numbers. There is little doubt that the majority of individuals find it easier to respond on a regular basis to a few key pieces of usually numerical information, which also provide a stimulus to seeking out further, more qualitative information if required. However, there will be a place for qualitative data-gathering and feedback, because it helps bring uncharted risks and unexpected opportunities to light.

Focusing upon the capture of quantifiable data, it is important to see the numbers to which individuals and organizations can respond as more than just financial information. Financial information alone cannot capture the extent of an organization's success in following its strategy or maintaining a high-energy connectedness with its marketplace. Kaplan and Norton[3] have suggested that the complexity of managing an organization today requires an ability to view performance in several areas simultaneously. They propose that feedback should focus on four basic questions:

- How do customers see us?
- What must we excel at?
- Can we continue to improve and create value?
- How do we look to our shareholders?

Answering these questions requires the creation of measures of four perspectives:

- customer satisfaction;
- internal processes;
- learning and innovation; and
- relevant financial performance data.

Every organization needs to determine which measures will be the most appropriate for them, within each of these perspectives, and also determine the most efficient method of collecting and maintaining data. The measures will be derived from orientation and strategy of the organization and the market conditions from which these have been derived. Many companies have adopted this 'balanced scorecard' approach and are using it to maintain external and internal connectedness. (An example of a scorecard is given in Fig. 8.3.)

In much of the literature on feedback there seems to be an implicit suggestion that this is a tool for senior management, or at least for management. A Renaissance approach, with its requirement for local responsiveness, clearly requires that the information available within a scorecard should be available to more or less everyone. As happened at the flour mill (see Chapter 4), hiding information from employees only develops misunderstanding and suspicion. It also needs to be translated at every level of the business, so that appropriate measures can be created upon which each individual's actions may have direct influence. For

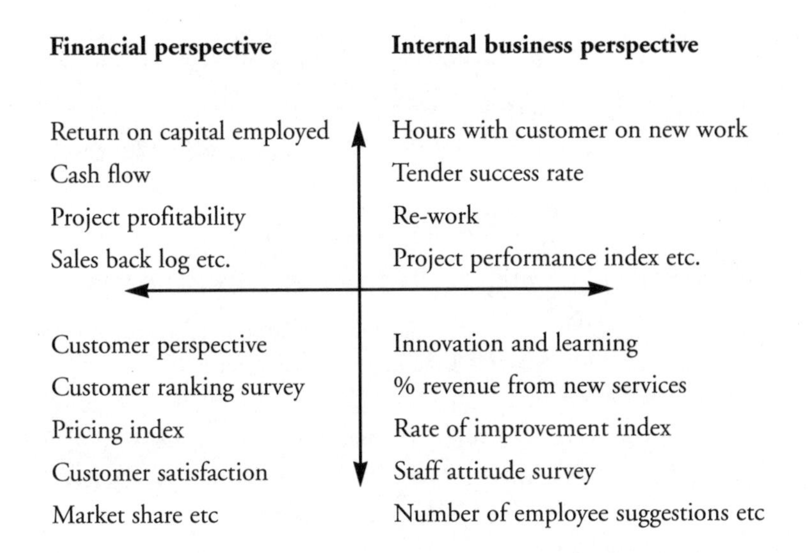

Fig. 8.3 Balanced scorecard: Rockwater (underwater engineering and construction)[4]

example, customer satisfaction feedback needs to refer not only to the organization as a whole, but also to those customers with whom a particular part of the business has dealings, or who can influence these particular scores.

CONNECTIONS: ENTERPRISE SYSTEMS

Many organizations are increasingly using integrated systems based upon software packages; these can handle all the information flowing through a company, including accounting, financial, supply-chain, HR, and customer information. The dream and goal is to make consistent information available where it is needed, connecting together different operating processes and activities. Packages such as R3, from German company SAP, can integrate a huge variety of data from accounts, executive information, personnel planning, payroll to inventory management, production planning, quality management, project management and sales planning. Often referred to as 'enterprise systems', these packages are in huge demand; the turnover of SAP in 1992 was $500m; by 1998 it was $3.3 billion.

In common with all connecting processes, management information systems come with the danger of over-integration and a constriction of diversity. Thomas Davenport, Professor at the Boston University School of Management, has declared that

> *an enterprise system by its very nature imposes its own logic on a company's strategy, organization and culture. It pushes a company toward full integration even when a certain degree of business unit segregation may be in its own best interests. And it pushes a company toward generic processes even when customized processes may be a source of competitive advantage.*[5]

This is a perfect example of the consistency/inconsistency dilemma highlighted in Chapter 1.

CONNECTEDNESS THROUGH LEARNING AND RISK MANAGEMENT

As highlighted in Fig. 8.2, a further aspect of information management systems is their potential to impact upon organizational learning and risk management. In many organizations, risk management and organizational learning are hampered by both implicit and explicit aspects of the power structure of the organization. This structure frequently inhibits or excludes local decision-making, driving it underground (see Chapter 11). The system fails to provide the means by which important feedback is communicated, consolidated and shared. As has been proposed, these two processes, because of the unpredictability of the markets and environment, share common features. For example, both depend upon getting immediate information from what is actually going on at any time, and need systems and structures that capture all this information, and make sure that it is rapidly communicated and shared. They both most often deal with probability rather than certainty. For both, therefore, an effective management information system could be very important.

Managing risk

It is probably reasonable to assume that, in most organizations, 95 per cent of risk can be managed through open access to information and by local decision-making. What is required is a protocol by which important risk, either threat or missed opportunity, can be escalated upwards within the organization, so that the organization can respond as a whole.

Every organization will have to create its own escalation protocol, deciding what information is needed and where, and at what level certain decisions must be made. Note that whatever particular structure and process is put in place, the measures of a balanced scorecard should provide a reference point for any escalation process. Certainly, all employees involved in a feedback and decision-making loop need to be able to express risk in terms of the value it represents to an organization, making it much more likely that it will be recognized, and a response will be made.

Capturing learning

How often does an organization re-invent the wheel? The creation of the best possible data-capture, communication and decision-making or problem-solving processes focuses organizations on both the changes in the environment, and the effectiveness of their response to it. Organizational learning, as opposed, say, to individual or local learning, is when a feedback loop is created, allowing data and decisions to be communicated for the benefit of the whole organization. Local data needs to be captured, and decisions must be made about its organizational level of importance, and, where necessary, communicated to other parts of the business. This learning model also allows organizations to see emerging patterns of market and environmental information by setting sequences of local data and decision-making alongside information from other sources. This is done both to establish when a more strategic response is needed, and where the laws of probability suggest that energy to create new interconnectedness might best be spent.

Of course, learning is more than the hearing or analysing of information. It is about acting on that information and learning from that experience. Organizational learning is therefore an active process, involving networking, negotiation, mentoring, and other aspects of connectedness. The sharing of learning may well be a role for a mentor or, indeed, a new expectation of managers.

CONNECTEDNESS THROUGH MENTORSHIP

Although information technology can go a long way to connecting an organization through a network, it is also important to develop human aspects of network-building and connectedness. One way would be to encourage movement between different jobs, to improve a sense of integration. In some organizations it might be useful to create a role of organizational 'mentor'; note that the term is not used here in the sense that is currently in vogue, which is almost synonymous with coach. The purpose of the mentor's role would be to challenge local thinking, communicate and reinforce company strategy and values, and also to gain understanding of a local perspective to communicate this both to the centre and to other local teams.

In organizations where there is much change, a mentor will be a force for continuity and the maintenance and sharing of experience. Such a person would join as a local team member, working on local projects and initiatives; after a while, he or she would move on. The Hong Kong Shanghai Banking Corporation (HSBC), one of the largest financial institutions in the world, is one organization that has been using a form of this role. It has a policy of maintaining a cadre of international officers who regularly move between different global locations, maintaining a tight network through which strategy and learning is disseminated and reinforced.

CONNECTIONS: INTEGRATION AND CONNECTEDNESS[6]

John Ridding has suggested in the *Financial Times* that HSBC's international officers have played a central part in the development of the bank, from a regional financier of colonial commerce to one of the most international and profitable financial institutions. The presence of the international officers, of which there are 400 out of a total of more than 30,000 employees in the bank, has helped to spread a strong culture throughout the group. As the bank builds a global operation, the system and its ability to adapt remain vital.

'They are the glue that sticks the fabric of a federal organization together,' says Chris Langley, general manager for Hong Kong and China.

CONNECTEDNESS THROUGH COMMUNICATION

I'll save you some money. In my desk drawer I have a management report on employee needs and attitudes in Ubiquitous Products and Services plc. Instead of paying an expensive management consultancy to undertake an extensive brief, you can have mine. Feel free to alter the name on the top. It will probably be 80 per cent accurate. The report will consist of one word: 'communication'.

The majority of attitude surveys seem to suggest that employees feel a serious lack of communication; in most cases, senior management, who have usually commissioned the survey, feel disappointed and even hurt. They point to newsletters, staff briefings, and even videos sent out in an effort to communicate with the rest of the business; but they forget what they have learnt from 'introduction to management' days, that communication is a two-way process. To be blunt, the front line staff need to be convinced that the senior team is on 'receive', before they will believe that they are credible enough to have anything to say. The front line is faced, day to day, with the reality of what the organization is trying to achieve, and needs to feel that the senior team acknowledges this. Much of the communication activity of senior managers, or of the top team, ought to be about listening rather than telling. The same is true of lateral communications around a business. Credibility will be all, and the pre-existence of a well-established network will also be vital.

Another problem with much organization communication is that, unless someone can see how the information affects him or her, and is in a position to react or respond to it in some way, it is not particularly meaningful to the recipient. It simply does not register as important. Communication would be greatly enhanced if a few simple conditions were put in place:

- There should be a clarity of purpose – why are we telling you this and how does is it linked to your present tasks and objectives?
- There should be clarity of expectation – an acknowledgement of what is expected of each party so that the recipient is clear about what it is that he/she is supposed to do or think differently as a result.
- There should be freedom of action – meeting the challenge of 'how much can I adapt what I have heard to meet the local conditions, which I understand and you probably don't?'

These suggestions apply as much to informal as to formal communications, and organizations should never underestimate the power of the network and role-modelling in the communication of what is important.

CONNECTIONS: EMPLOYEE COMMUNICATION GOOD PRACTICE

A survey by the Industrial Society[7] identified the following as important features if an organization wants to demonstrate good practice:

- A clear mission and values.
- A communication policy that reflects these values and describes the way it communicates within the organization as well as outside it.
- Regular surveys and audits of employees' views.
- An induction scheme, which gives an understanding of the whole organization.
- Systems for continual communication of reference items.
- The distribution of management information, and so on, in an orderly way so that people can categorize the messages they receive.
- Regular journals and newsletters as appropriate.
- Established communication standards for meetings, presentations and written communication.
- Minimum standards for one-to-one meetings.
- A system for team briefing.
- A system for gaining feedback on performance, changes, and so on.
- All-staff meetings once or twice a year for strategic priorities and context.
- A system allowing for employee questioning.
- Where major change is envisaged, communication should be planned in as part of the process, and should be two-way.
- Ongoing consultation.
- Mechanisms allowing people to present their ideas directly to decision-makers.

- An encouragement of lateral communication through working groups, tasks forces, social contacts, and networks.
- Senior managers regularly 'walking the job', talking directly with employees.

Connectedness and Climate

In a world where a small detail can make a big difference, a computer-based information system will not always highlight the critical elements that need attention. What is required is a heightened sense of awareness – a sort of organizational early-warning system based upon hunches and intuition. This will have to depend less on technology than on people. One way this can be achieved is through the organizational mentors, but really every individual needs to be a potential radar for changes.

These issues will be particularly important for qualitative and rogue information. Organizations need to encourage individuals who can spot key information as it emerges and wrinkles the smooth strategic horizon. Individuals also need to feel a sense of responsibility to do something with this information, even if does not directly concern their job. This sense of responsibility lies outside the strict definitions of a job description and relies instead on an individual wanting to act. This will depend upon the culture and climate of the organization. An atmosphere of trust, openness and lack of fear would seem to favour this. It is not unusual for an individual who sees difficulties or problems not to say anything, for fear of being branded a trouble-maker. People will also fail to speak if they feel they are not valued, or even listened to.

Climate will also directly affect the extent to which a person identifies with an organization and is, therefore, prepared to commit to it. Organizations should identify those positive aspects of their collective identity or 'personality' (the organizational brand), and emphasize it in everything that they do. This is something that Richard Branson's Virgin Group seems to do startlingly well, with the consequent benefits to both employee and organization.

Connectedness through ownership

Arguably, ownership could be a force for connectedness. If connectedness is about hearts as well as minds, then a sense of belonging, and identification driven by linking an individual to an organization's overall and longer-term performance through shareholding, seems to be a useful force for connectedness.

Evidence of the impact of this was discussed in the *Observer*,[8] which quoted finance house Capital Strategies' index of 30 companies in which more than 10 per cent of issued capital is held by or for employees. The index seems to offer evidence of a link between employee ownership and corporate performance, with the index rising threefold between 1992 and 1997, beating the FTSE All Share Index by 89 per cent. While the direct causal link with share ownership is still far from proven, there is growing empirical evidence that share ownership and shareholder value go together. A much bigger sample of US companies, using the same methodology as the UK index, showed an identical result: far from destroying shareholder value, spreading ownership among employees can substantially help investor returns.

As yet, UK companies have been relatively reluctant to include employees outside the boardroom in share-ownership schemes. One notable exception is the John Lewis Partnership, the UK retailer that is wholly owned by its employees. However, it might be that a greater distribution of share ownership is forced upon organizations in a bid to maintain the loyalty of 'knowledge workers'. These people possess the intellectual capital that is fast becoming the real value of a company.

Connectedness through networks and negotiations

One of the results of the sense of belonging will be the emergence of strong networks. As suggested previously, networks are what make organizations work. They can sustain bad, old organizational structures and systems long after the conditions that created those structures and systems have waned. Networks may also enable bad, new structures and systems to survive. However, within a Renaissance approach, networks are more than the way structures and systems are enabled; they actually are those structures and systems.

Networks also provide evidence of the self-organizing and adaptive capability of complex systems. Those who wish to shape organizations, in pursuit of strategic goals, will be better rewarded by promoting the behaviour and permissions that are necessary to establish effective and spontaneous networks than by attempting to create them directly by external intervention. Promoting such behaviour will be a brave but key step. Will organizations allow networks to form, allow them time to meet, and allow them the resources to pursue their goals? Before an organization prevents this happening, it should ask what it is in the system that is creating the need for that network to establish itself. It could be reflecting a hidden but vital impulse for organizational success. The challenge for the organization is to go with the flow.

One of the ways that an organization might promote the necessary behaviour for the spontaneous establishment of networks is by having mentors or managers responsible for creating and facilitating forums. These could arise from the needs of the people in the organization to connect. In these issues, needs and interests can be discussed, challenged and defended, and innovative solutions can be sought. Such networks and forums for negotiation would allow people to respond to the experience they have of the work challenge and take responsibility for the future of their organizations.

CONNECTEDNESS BY MANAGEMENT

Most of the above ideas for connectedness will need a guardian angel to maintain and promote them. This is Renaissance Management, and the considerations for this are discussed fully in Chapters 11 and 12.

SUMMARY

There is no one best way to connect up an organization so that there is alignment between it, its market and its employees (and other stakeholders). Each organization will find its own solution, including perhaps its oldest connection of all – just telling everyone what to do. Whatever mix of techniques is used will determine very much how the team and management issues discussed in the next chapter are enacted.

REFERENCES

1. Nohria, N and Ghoshal, S (1997) *The Differentiated Network*, Jossey Bass, California.
2. Nohria, N and Ghoshal, S, ibid.
3. Kaplan, R S and Norton, D P (Jan/Feb 1992) The balanced scorecard – measures that drive performance, *Harvard Business Review.*
4. Kaplan, R S and Norton, D P (Sept/Oct 1993) Putting the balanced scorecard to work, *Harvard Business Review.*
5. Davenport, T H (July/August 1998) Putting the enterprise into the enterprise system, *Harvard Business Review.*
6. Ridding, J (1997) The ties that bind, the *Financial Times*, 25 April.
7. Industrial Society (1994) *Managing best practice – the regular benchmark (Employee communications)*, Industrial Society, London.
8. Caulkin, S (1997) Footloose and fancying a share of the profits, *Observer*, 15 June.

CHAPTER 9

BUILDING THE RENAISSANCE TEAM

ARE TEAMS ALWAYS NEEDED?

ONE OF the assumptions of Renaissance Management is that teams can contribute not just to organizational performance but provide the essential forum in which the potential synergy that exists in and between individuals with collective responsibility for an organizational result will be best realized. The challenge is to create teams that can maximally contribute to an organization within the operating realities of today and the future. To do this, teams have to be places in which individuals want and are able to contribute in the most effective ways. They should not feel blocked because they are not allowed to or do not have the skills to offer all they could to the team and thereby their organization.

Of course, part of the challenge will be to create teams in which members also want, and feel, motivated to contribute as extensively as possible.

Teams therefore should be seen as one of the key forums in which energy is practically exchanged within an organization. Most organizations have stories about teams which seemed to do extraordinary things and whose members felt transformed by it. For many of us thinking about our careers to date can recall being a member of a team which achieved great success and left us energized – either through the profile it gave us, the development it offered or by the continuing pleasure and pride it gives us to recall being a member of *that* team at that time.

What is it that an organization should therefore focus on to ensure that it has done all it can to create high-energy/high-performing teams through which to pursue its goals? There seem to be three areas or levels of concern which will impact upon team effectiveness:

1. The external environment of the team and the outputs it is expected to deliver;
2. The team climate that establishes what it is like to be a member of a particular team; and
3. Finally, the way that individuals can contribute to a team.

The rest of this chapter will deal with the first level of concern – the external world of the team, what might be expected of it and what considerations should be given in terms of the availability and allocation of resources. Chapter 10 will deal with the more internal aspects of the challenge in terms of team climate and expectations of individual contribution.

Before turning to any of this it is important to clearly position teams within organizations – why and when they are useful and also when other structures might be sought.

A major assumption of this book is that teams are a primary feature of a Renaissance Organization, so it may seem perverse at this stage to question whether they are always needed. There is confusion about what a team is, although the consensus is that they are 'a good thing'. Employees are exhorted to act as one big team, and senior managers, even when they are busy building personal empires and undermining others, are often called the 'top team'. (Sometimes it looks more like they are playing different games rather than playing on the same side in the same game.) Wherever one person gets to talk regularly to another, a 'team' is declared. This is probably because team-working has become an espoused value of many organizations – something that is important because it reinforces corporate identity and, hopefully, encourages all to work for the greater good. This value does not need to be defended at the outset of this chapter, but the role of the team as the key structural element (or basic work unit) of an organization does.

Teams seem to belong to more stable, predictable times, when they have more time to form properly. Times when they can develop effective and efficient ways of operating over relatively long-term time periods; the effectiveness and efficiency are achieved through a clear differentiation of roles undertaken in a climate of close co-operation and mutual support. Certainly, it can be maintained that teams built upon these assumptions will find it difficult to operate in the current environment, particularly in view of the fact that the instability of team membership seems inevitably to arise in times of rapid change.

Furthermore, it is arguable that teams like these are the last thing a flexible and innovative organization needs. Teams can be a force for cohesion and integration, or almost a form of coercion. Teams quickly develop the assumptions and values that encourage members to fit in. Therefore, if teams are created to reflect the corporate perspectives, as transmitted from top management, teams may suppress innovation and be insufficiently radical.

Whatever teams are about, it is not stability and conformity. Nor are they the solution to all organizational design problems. There will be plenty of room for individual action in Renaissance Organizations. One of the challenges will be to reconcile an individual's need and desire to make decisions and create solutions for him or herself with the responsibilities of team membership.

Building and maintaining teams requires an ongoing commitment of resource. As with all investments, it is worth establishing when the return on the investment is likely to be too low to make the investment worthwhile. Therefore, it is also worth noting those circumstances in which the creation of teams is not worthwhile, as follows:

- when tasks are relatively simple;
- where the tasks are more difficult but have few elements or operations, which can be handled by one person, or by several, if there is

only a limited need for co-ordination of effort or communication;
- when the number of decisions that need to be taken by the team as a whole is very small;
- when individual decisions have little impact upon others; for example, when people in an organization are grouped together for administrative rather than strategic reasons – it is not unusual to find a group of people in one department who represent, respectively, office services, health and safety, and perhaps, in smaller organizations, IT.

In short, teams should only exist where it can be proved that the whole will be greater than the sum of the parts.

When are teams needed?

Teams are not always essential, therefore, but in certain conditions they are vital. Teams are essential if knowledge workers are to work together and co-ordinate their specialized and cross-functional skills. The question is not whether teams are important but, rather, how, when and under what assumptions teams can contribute either energy gain or energy efficiency to an organization. From a Renaissance point of view, this will be about releasing the energy held in the differences as well as the similarities that exist in a group of people, in terms of perspectives, ideas and experience, enabling them to innovate and have an impact on important goals. The benefits of effective team behaviour would be especially useful ways of establishing or supporting local adaptivity, innovation and energy gain in the following circumstances:

- complex situations needing to be approached from more than one perspective;
- projects or tasks with uncertainty or low levels of predictability;
- when diverse stakeholders need to be included; and
- when first-class communication or co-ordination is essential.

One of the assumptions of Renaissance Management is that teams are able not just to contribute to organizational performance, but also to provide an essential forum. It is in such a forum that the potential synergy that exists in and between the individuals with collective responsibility for an organizational result will be best realized.

WHAT ARE TEAMS REALLY LIKE?

Consultants seem unable to resist analogies, and in the field of teams and team development we really go to town. Organizational teams have been described as being like SAS units, an aerobatics display squadron, the pit-lane team in Formula One racing, a Five Nations rugby union team, and, quite disturbingly, medical staff in an operating theatre! Most of these analogies are not as relevant as they could be. The examples used have the opportunity for rehearsal and, in most cases, the team members have well-defined parts to play. Indeed, the idea of spontaneously changing procedure in an aerobatics team, for example, would be downright dangerous. In modern organizations there is little time for rehearsal (perhaps there should be, but in an unpredictable world it would be a difficult and perhaps wasteful thing to attempt), and individuals and teams have to respond on intuition and gut feeling.

Furthermore, common to these analogies is an emphasis on a close-knit team being developed over a period of time, with a stability of membership that is not always possible within organizations. Lastly, these analogies, which reflect many deeply held assumptions about teams, are characterized by a clarity of goal and a limited set of expectations. Such teams operate within a well-defined field – for example, a pit crew would be bewildered if a stagecoach and four pulled into the pit, and the hospital crew might be baffled if they were asked to operate on an elephant.

A Renaissance team is able to operate in a much wider field of concern, in which expectations can change in unforeseen ways. It is good practice for a team to have a focused clarity of purpose and a limited set of expectations, but is it possible in a highly volatile environment? How often in organizations do individuals have to tackle unexpected areas, or create additional or alternative goals to fulfil the overall purpose of the team? One of the most important insights that I have gained from working with teams – particularly those responsible for implementing strategic change – is the extent to which they have to negotiate and establish expectations, and the extent of their field of concern.

This experience suggests that teams are a much more dynamic structure than some of the work that has been done in this area would imply. (See Connections, below, for a summary of these perceptions.)

CONNECTIONS: WHAT TEAMS ARE REALLY LIKE

Over the last few years, I have been working with numerous teams at middle to senior management levels within an organization. A number of characteristics have become increasingly common features of these teams. Of these I would highlight the following:

- teams have to negotiate to establish what their goals and ways of working should be, although it often takes a little time for them to realize this;
- the lifespan of different teams will vary considerably and that team membership is almost constantly changing;
- unlike some previous team models, which emphasized clear identification of roles and strict adherence to procedures, there is a growing need to improvise/innovate;
- following from the above point, individuals have more than one role in these teams;
- people are often members of more than one team and this can create situations of divided loyalties;
- there should be a bias for change – teams are created as much to fathom the future as to maintain the now.

Team challenges

Teams, then, have to operate in a world that is far more complex than has generally been supposed. Part of this complexity is the differing expectations an organization can have of particular teams.

What is expected of teams can differ in two broad ways. Teams can be asked to work in established or new ways, and they can be asked to work for established or new goals in terms of outputs. For example, an organization may introduce team-working in order to improve efficiency or productivity in the manufacture or supply of established products or services. Alternatively, it may use an established team to use established processes and ways of working in pursuit of new outputs. Furthermore, a team might be asked to find new ways of working together in pursuit of new outputs. Lastly, team-working might be based on existing processes and existing goals. (Confusingly of course, you could talk of teams having the output of introducing new processes but here I am referring to the tasks the team faces, ie what the team has to do rather than how.) The position is summarized in Fig. 9.1.

	Established outputs	New outputs
Established processes	Maintenance teams	Project teams
New processes	Efficiency teams	Pathfinder teams

Fig. 9.1 Team challenges

From the point of view of the organization, teams in the shaded area in Fig. 9.1 are strategically being asked to help the organization meet its market in different ways. Those in the unshaded area help an organization to meet its market in better ways. Critically, differences will occur between the team types, in terms of the degree of uncertainty in which they have to operate and, related to this, in the amount of innovation that will be required.

Maintenance teams

Maintenance teams need to operate in a relatively stable environment, in which any changes to what they are expected to do, and how they are expected to do it, will be incremental. A key question for these sort of teams will be whether they are required at all; and, if so, how may levels of motivation and commitment be maintained? A significant feature of this will be in the individual needs of the team members, and the possibility of structuring the work to increase the intrinsic rewards of doing it. Such teams may suit self-management and, properly established, can support a move away from control to more autonomy. A shop-floor self-managed team is an example of a maintenance team.

Efficiency teams

Efficiency teams are often concerned with continuous improvements, including changes to processes in order to reduce costs, reduce errors or speed up production. Examples of efficiency teams include those responsible for the introduction of total quality management, and those looking at more radical changes to process. The danger in such teams is that, without strategic leadership, they can find better and better ways of producing the wrong thing. Depending on their remit, quality circles might be an example of either maintenance groups or efficiency groups.

CONNECTIONS: ELITE (ELIMINATING THE ERRORS) TEAMS

Jon Katzenbach and Douglas Smith[1] have made a study of over 50 teams in many different organizations. Among their results were a number of general findings, including the fact that:

- high-performing teams were extremely rare; and
- teams were the primary unit of performance for increasing numbers of organizations.

Among the many examples quoted, one that seems to provide a clear example of an efficiency team is the Elite team on the *Talahassee Democrat.* This team was charged with improving the paper's woeful record on the quality of its advertising – its lifeblood. Advertisers complained of errors, unresponsiveness, too many internal procedures, and an unwillingness of anyone to take responsibility for problems. Within a year, the Elite team delivered a 99 per cent accuracy rate, lost revenues were reduced from $10,000 per month to virtually zero, and advertiser satisfaction rates soared.

A number of processes seemed to come together to produce this result:

- after some early difficulties, a climate of emotional openness was achieved in the team;
- there was focus and clarity about the challenge; and
- a high level of personal commitment developed.

Assumptions were challenged and innovations sought. For example, people selling the adverts were given fax machines and mobile phones to allow the ads to be sent to the paper and processed throughout the day rather than in a rush at five o'clock as had been the case.

Project teams

Project teams employ tried and trusted processes to meet new goals. Typically, they will be drawn from different functions or areas of operation, and individuals will contribute largely from the perspective of the function from which they have been drawn. In some organizations, such teams have been used to help set strategy. One function will usually dominate, and the leader will be drawn from that function. This functional perspective is likely to carry with it implicit assumptions about the role of each team member, and there may be little scope for contributing beyond that assumed role.

Within a defined domain or area of operation, in which it is felt that familiar rules apply, project teams can effectively meet new outputs. However, there is always the danger that old assumptions are inappropriately applied to new and subtly different problems. On more than one occasion, I have worked with very large organizations that have tried to apply project team-working to a situation that really demanded a pathfinder team approach. The result is usually inappropriate processes being applied to a challenge that looks deceptively familiar. There is a similar risk with another type of project team – R&D teams. If R&D teams use a similar range of processes in all their work, it is likely that the outputs will be variations on a theme; this is only acceptable if it is what the market-place requires.

Pathfinder teams

As a rule of thumb, project teams offer cross-functional representation, while pathfinder teams try to achieve cross-functional working. Pathfinder teams are truly autonomous and the fullest expression of local adaptivity. Within an agreed strategic framework, they are left to establish the goals and processes that will work best for them at local level.

The challenge facing pathfinder teams at the outset is that they only have a general idea of where they are going, and only a vague map of how they are going to get there. The destination, also referred to as the 'vision', may not even be their own, but something that is almost intuitively 'felt' by another, who may find it difficult to specify exactly what the destination might look like. They are therefore faced with two problems: to discover exactly what is required from a general set of co-ordinates, and to find the appropriate processes to get there. Such teams may well have to think outside of their own functional 'box' and find innovative and sometimes radical ways to work together.

Pathfinder groups can arise as the result of a particular department or service in a business finding itself classified as a profit centre. They may also be the result of a re-engineering project that leads to a more customer-focused way of working. As well as existing in situations of ongoing responsibility, they can also be created with much shorter timespans to meet particular challenges. This may be necessary in a crisis or in response to a significant but unexpected event in the market-place.

Pathfinder teams are, in my experience, scarcely recognized in organizations at the moment, yet they will become more and more apparent as the nature of the challenges they face are better understood. Without this recognition, there is a danger that the needs of such teams will not be properly resourced. In particular, it is likely that the climate in which they operate will not be conducive to their obtaining the results needed by the organization.

CONNECTIONS: IDENTIFYING PATHFINDER TEAMS

In work undertaken with supply chain re-engineering teams, I found that one of the issues which took a little while for teams to identify was that they were pathfinder teams. They largely operated as project teams contributing from a functional standpoint. Part of the problem was identifying what the output was. In this case it was not just the manufactured items but the central work-flow system itself. Although the supply chain had been described in overall terms, a key output for the teams was the detail and practical implications of the system. This therefore required innovation around the processes within the team that would make, both the establishing and running of the system, possible. The consequence of this was that a great deal more in the way of negotiation, resourcing and structuring had to occur than was immediately apparent and the teams were the ones in the only position to drive this forward.

All four types of team will exist within Renaissance Organizations and all will need to find the best way of contributing positively to energy creation. The trick will be for teams to recognize the sort of challenge being faced, in terms of goals and processes, and insist that there is agreement upon them. For example, a group may be given the goal of improving processes when the market is actually suggesting that new outputs are required. This is an example of how goals can become distorted, leading to a great waste of energy. This suggests that teams can move between these four positions and emphasizes the need for autonomy and negotiation.

Operating climate

The term 'operating climate' should not be confused with 'team climate' discussed in Chapter 10. It is an overarching term to include all the practical, political and emotional support a team will need if it is to succeed. Although the term describes the climate in fairly instrumental terms, it is also aware of all aspects of the working environment of the team.

Fundamentally, the operating climate of the team can be characterized by the degree of autonomy which a team has over what it is trying to achieve, and how it is trying to achieve it. Within a specific organization and set of market conditions, the 'requisite autonomy' of a team needs to be defined.

Requisite autonomy is the level of autonomy in which a group needs to operate, in order to achieve its results. If there is too much autonomy, there is a real danger that the results will not accord with the needs of the organization as a whole; if there is too little, the team is unable to do anything differently, and therefore the synergy within the team cannot be properly exploited. Teams involved with change need space in which to problem-solve and make decisions. This space is created in two ways; by organizations allowing the team to operate to an extent outside the normal constraints and procedures that bind the everyday life of an organization together, and through the team's ability to express its own individuality.

Pathfinder teams, in particular, are charged with finding ways in which to do things differently, but how often do organizations consider these aspects of permission when they create teams to do new things? Too often, it seems that they ask for teams to pursue the radical, to make waves, and then are surprised when the boat starts to rock. Clearly, what a team does, and how it does it, needs to be circumscribed in some way. However, this should be a matter for discussion and planning, otherwise the results can be extremely difficult; the ultimate risk is that the team might leave the organization to pursue its own vision.

In more detail, requisite autonomy asks a question about how free teams are, in terms of their control of:

- resources;
- goals; and
- processes.

Each of these key areas can be subdivided (see Fig. 9.1) and the degree of autonomy required over each needs to be established. Fig. 9.2 shows one team's report on levels of autonomy in a pathfinder challenge. The data shows the team's perceptions of autonomy in the key area of resource. It contrasts levels of resource available to the team with the team's ability to control the allocation of that resource. The balance between control and autonomy needs to be appropriate to the challenge faced by a particular team, and the suggestion here is that the greater the need for innovation, the greater the need for autonomy. The ability of teams to determine these areas will have a crucial impact on their ability to contribute, to innovate and to adapt to create a high-energy organization.

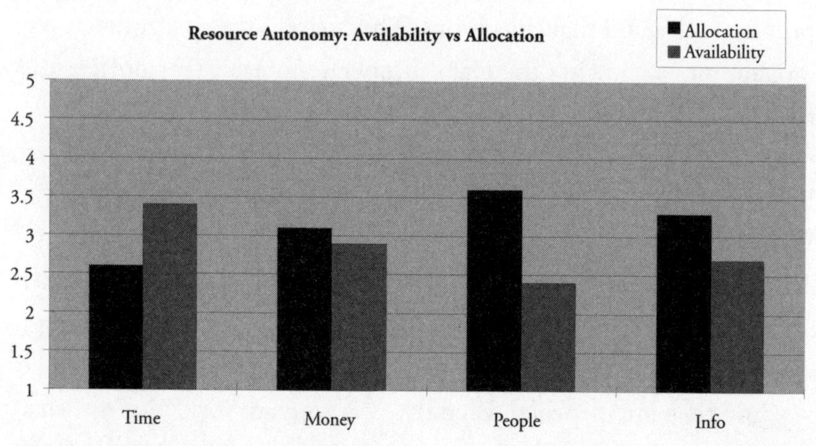

This data shows a team's perceptions of autonomy in the key area of resources. It contrasts levels of resource availability to the team with the team's ability to control the allocation of that resource.

Fig. 9.2 Resource autonomy

Establishing requisite autonomy

If there is a psychological contract between individual and employer, there also needs to be one between an organization and its different teams. This contract will be tested whenever things get difficult. It is easy, as reality bites, for nerves to fail, and this is often expressed in a withdrawal of resources (including control over decision-making). This tendency can be lessened if the autonomy of the team is counterbalanced, not by control but by connectedness, as described in Chapter 8. Of particular importance will be timely and accurate feedback on progress and the visible support of senior management.

Table 9.1 Dimensions of operating climate © IDE 1997

Dimensions of a team operating climate

Resource autonomy

To deliver results, teams will need to have an understanding of the resources they need to have available to achieve their goals. This can be divided into two different aspects: resource availability, and the extent to which the group can control its allocation. For example, there may be plenty of finance available for a project, but the group may believe that it has little discretion or control over how it is spent. Key areas identified for resource are time, money, people and information.

Process autonomy

Communication is concerned with how a team interacts, both with each other and with others, to give and receive information, offer and gain opinions, and so on. Its impact will be felt in the ways in which a team can manage its own PR, and go about gaining support for its ideas and decisions. Internal structuring is concerned with the way the task and sub-tasks are divided, and individual responsibilities are allocated and undertaken. Decision-making is an essential part of team life. To an extent, decision-making will be affected by team resource autonomy, but there is actually a much wider field of decision-making possibilities potentially open to a team. Linked to internal structuring, the dimension work process is concerned with the freedom a team has to instigate the internal business processes that it uses. (For example, must it use formal project-planning or established review techniques?)

Goal autonomy

Goal autonomy relates to the extent to which a team can set its own goals and outputs. There are two types of goals under consideration here. Results goals are the way in which the success or otherwise of the team will ultimately be measured. Output goals are decisions about what exactly the team is trying to achieve, and how they are going to do it. On many occasions, all these decisions will be set by the organization; sometimes, very few of them will, beyond some overall financial contribution.

Connectedness

Connectedness deals with the strength and visibility of a number of factors that integrate an organization without placing the burden of over-control on the operation of teams. It needs to be measured from four different perspectives:

- instrumental, providing feedback through management information systems;
- socio-emotional, through measures of climate;
- negotiated – identified by the existence and use of forums for debate and co-ordination; and
- power, measured through senior-management access and support.

Overall connectedness will be driven by shared vision.

SUMMARY

This chapter deals with the aspects external to the team that will affect its ability to deliver a high-energy contribution to an organization. It suggests the importance of being clear about the nature of the challenge faced by a particular team, and understanding the implications of that challenge in terms of the way that team will have to work. Getting the right balance between control and autonomy is of central importance to the success of any team, to ensure that the team can take the decisions it needs to take, and that it has the resources it needs in order to implement those decisions.

REFERENCE

1. Katzenbach, J R and Smith, D K (1993) *The Wisdom of Teams*, Harvard Business School Press, Boston.

CHAPTER 10

RELEASING THE ENERGY – MAXIMIZING TEAM CONTRIBUTION

HAVING HIGHLIGHTED in the previous chapter those factors external to the team – the nature of the outputs it is expected to deliver and the operating climate in which it is expected to deliver them – it is now time to examine the ways in which a group of people can combine if they are to create the levels of energy, innovation and flexibility needed to deliver these outputs. This will mean focusing on the other two areas of analysis: the team climate and individual contribution.

The relationship between external environment, team climate and individual behaviour is obviously intimate and important to understand if an organization is to create teams who can fulfil their part in creating a high-energy environment. This is why the second level concept of team climate is so valuable, because team effectiveness is not just a result of external factors, such as outcome required, resources etc, or the motivation and behaviours of team members, but a result of the interaction of both. Team climate defines what sort of team it is, what behaviours will be encouraged and discouraged and the extent to which individuals feel their needs can be met and thereby the extent to which they feel committed.

It can be argued that there are several components to team climate that will determine team effectiveness:

- vision;
- constructive conflict;
- playfulness;
- trust and support;
- collective individualism;
- entrepreneurial finish.

In almost all these components, it is possible to recognize both internal and external facing aspects: internal aspects concerning the relationships of team members; and external aspects concerning how they go about achieving their tasks. This can be demonstrated most clearly by looking at the first component of team climate – vision.

VISION

Vision occurs both as an important factor in the internal life of the team and as fundamental to its ability to deliver an external result. A vision that was purely internally focused – to be the happiest team in the company, say – might be great for interpersonal relationships but not exactly guaranteed to contribute to the bottom line. On the other hand a vision that was 'grow by 250 per cent p.a.', which did not have the emotional support of the team, or any real sense of commitment to it, runs the risk of not being achieved. Vision must, in its implications, look both ways – in terms of what it means to the team and to the market-place. In this way it catalyses a high-energy contribution at all levels. A team that was high on interpersonal skills but low on enterprise would be a comfortable place to be, while the opposite may at first be exciting, but in the long term runs the risk of being interpersonally destructive. It is when they both come together that real high performing teams can start to function.

This is an area which has been studied in depth by Neil Anderson and Michael West,[1] who have developed considerable insights into the way effective teams work and, in particular, innovate. Their model straddles both the internal and external facing aspects of high performing/high energy teams and is a useful reminder that in reality the two are intimately related.

Team vision, they point out, is not just a matter of whether a team has one, but how team members perceive it. The first question that needs to be addressed is to what extent the vision of the team is understood and recognized by all the team. They would argue that it is not necessary for a vision to be articulated, and it may be implicit in a team's actions – influencing a team's ability to change and innovate far more than a poorly defined, artificially created one. Vision, they also suggest, should be shared and negotiated if members can pool their collective energies and creativity to secure the most effective and efficient results.

In addition to this, a team also needs to think about 'visioning', ie the process of building a vision. In an unpredictable and volatile world, blindly following a vision that ignores the changes and reality around it is fanaticism. Teams need the ability to adapt and build a vision together that reflects both their ambition and their experience.

CONSTRUCTIVE CONFLICT

A productive team climate is not necessarily a place of polite reserve – in fact one of the important dimensions in Anderson and West's work is 'appraisal'. This concerns the ability of team members to critically reflect upon their team's performance and to challenge assumptions, standards, 'the way we do things round here' etc. This is something that is found in few teams, yet without it, there is a danger of 'group think' – a pressure to respond to the world in the same way, low creativity and poor decision-making. Teams can elevate consensus as a value, far above the contribution it can make to the business. It is therefore worth considering for a moment the role of conflict and controversy in teams. Traditionally this has been regarded as undesirable, but in fact it is probably inevitable and certainly essential for superior teamwork. Conflict is important because, as Gareth Morgan says in *Images of Organisation*,[2] it can:

> *energize an organization. Conflict counters tendencies towards lethargy, staleness, apathetic compliance and similar organizational pathologies, by creating a 'keep on your toes' atmosphere where it is dangerous to take things for granted.*

We know from the work of Apter discussed in Chapter 5 that everyone is motivated to challenge, to question, to conflict sometimes with the ideas, assumptions and direction of a team. The question is, what sort of conflict? What is required in a team is not an atmosphere of negativity, undermining each other, but conflict, which takes place in an atmosphere of trust and co-operation to enable a full examination of a problem or challenge. This allows consensual decisions to be made, ie not compromise decisions, but real decisions based on a multi-perspective view. Dean Tjosvold[3] has called this 'constructive controversy', stating that:

> *Controversy, when discussed in a co-operative context, stimulates elaboration of views, the search for new information and ideas and the integration of apparently opposing positions. These dynamics result in understanding the problem, more adequate solutions, and commitment to implement them.*

It is the surfacing of these differences rather than their suppression that creates the energy and focus that allows a team to succeed. Again we are faced with high levels of social skills or emotional intelligence being a vital part of successful team membership.

Connections: Encouraging Controversy

Dorothy Leonard and Susan Straus,[4] in arguing for diversity within organizations, have highlighted the hiring practices of Nissan Design who hire their designers in 'virtual pairs', ie when they hire a designer who 'glories in the freedom of pure colour and rhythm', they will next hire a 'very rational, Bauhaus-trained designer who favours analysis and focuses on function'.

Playfulness

Given an operating environment that demands maximum return on resources, that imposes ever more stretching targets, then there is no doubt about it; work is a very serious business. Encouraging teams to be playful would therefore seem to be a non-starter. However, the benefits of playfulness in terms of its impact on creativity and exploration have been highlighted by those working in Reversal Theory and from other perspectives. In working with several teams myself belonging to very serious companies, it is generally the case that initially they find any discussion of playfulness awkward and inhibiting. If, however, there is the chance to work with these teams and make them more comfortable with appropriate play then the impact on both quality and quantity of ideas and innovations they identify can be quite astonishing.

E K A Nobell, a large Swedish chemical company, was studied in depth by Nystrom[5] to determine the impact of climate and culture on innovative performance. What was found was that the most innovative division of the company was also the one that rated most highly in terms of its 'playfulness'. The empirical research carried out by Nystrom also highlighted aspects of creative conflict in that the most innovative division also encouraged freedom, challenge, risk-taking and debate.

TRUST AND SUPPORT

The way that successful teams work is underpinned by one fundamental – trust. It is hard to imagine any sort of team operating successfully in which trust was missing or less than well developed. Trust allows for conflicts, which are essential to effective team functioning, to be raised in a positive and collaborative way. Trust allows for the free flow of information and openness about difficulties. Trust means that team members feel supported. It is a prerequisite of teams being able to take risks that there is trust between team members built on a recognition of each other's commitment and contribution.

Normally trust and support like this are built up through shared experience – experience that is deliberately planned for and developed over a period of time, particularly in the armed services, for example. Unfortunately this is precisely the environment that is missing in modern organizations, where teams are brought together for relatively short periods of time and, particularly at more senior levels, where people are expected to be members of several teams. The challenge will be to develop ways in which this trust can be built more rapidly and an effective level of understanding quickly reached (see team joining, below).

COLLECTIVE INDIVIDUALISM

An important feature of team climate, and one that seems overlooked in most discussions about team performance, is the interface between individual action and group control. Essentially this is a local example of the consistency/inconsistency dilemma – what is the control vs autonomy balance?

Of course there are two levels at which a need for autonomy is an important issue for a team:

1. at the level of the team and the environment (operating climate) in which it operates; and

2. between the different individual members within a team.

This first example is the 'requisite autonomy' discussed earlier, but interestingly the same issue applies at the intra-team level, ie to what extent can individuals operate autonomously within the team – allocating resources, taking decisions or actions on behalf of but without direct reference to it? This is a subtle area of contracting that must be implicitly understood before a team can operate successfully, and is particularly pertinent to teams that can only meet as a total group occasionally. The importance of intra-team autonomy is not just important in building group harmony but is a matter of defining the way in which the team will pursue its goals and get its results. It will depend on the climate of the team and the characteristics of individuals within it. Borrowing the vocabulary of Colin Hastings: the quality required can be characterized as 'collective individualism', ie *needing to be independent, wanting to collaborate.* A team will have to work out how to deal with these issues at a very practical level. It is likely that having established operating levels of autonomy, agreements on norms and processes such as decision-making will have to be established. The team will also have to deal with those who operate outside these agreed levels of autonomy.

ENTREPRENEURIAL FINISH

So far our discussion has centred on the internal processes and conditions that help a team work well. Left at this level, there is a sense that we could be developing teams that are enormously self-sufficient, but that are not really contributing too much to an organization. Teams that exist within organizations are there to achieve a result. To an extent, the ways and means of doing this are imposed upon maintenance and project teams, but efficiency teams and especially pathfinder teams have to take responsibility for how they are going to achieve their results. What is demanded of these teams is some entrepreneurial finish, ie not just the ability to think or create the means they require to deliver their goals, or

CONNECTIONS: DECISION-MAKING

I have found it useful in working with several teams and focusing on this issue to get them to clarify who can make what sort of decisions. In doing so the team has clarified what, if any, decisions can be made, in each of three categories:

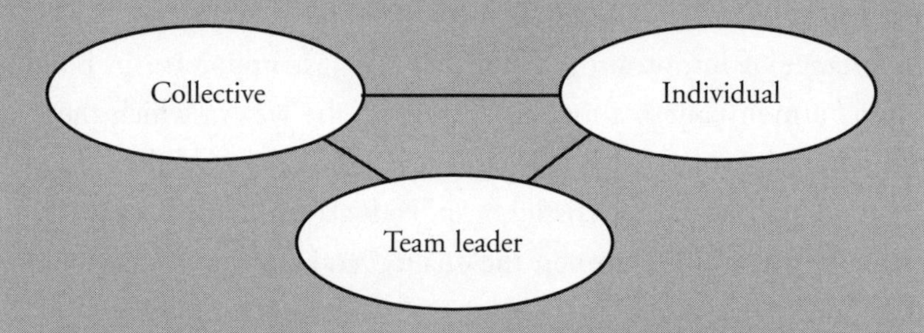

Fig. 10.1 Decision-making categories

Often this stimulates a discussion which highlights many assumptions both about the purpose of the team and the role of individuals within it. It challenges the team and the team leader to be absolutely clear about the decisions only the team leader can make – albeit often through discussions with the rest of the team. It also identifies those decisions, if any, in which the team leader assumes no more authority than any other team member, and finally those decisions that should be taken outside the context of a collective response but which perhaps are reported to the others for information. The debate has been valuable at front-line and board level!

just the ability to innovate, ie engineer the idea into a workable format, but added to these the skills and behaviours that will see them successfully implemented within an organization. This is the final hurdle at which many teams fail. The solution to a particular problem or challenge, it seems, can be solved by a balance, *in abstract,* but once introduced into the messy, political, unfair world of organizational reality, it fails.

Part of entrepreneurial finish will be driven by the extent to which team members individually find the team's outputs personally important. Firstly, it is reasonable to propose that the greater the extent to which team members feel their own personal needs can be met by the team succeeding, the more they will invest in that success. Such individual needs may be about reward and status, but they may also be about learning and development, helping others etc – in fact many of the different motivational states identified in Reversal Theory (see Chapter 5. Not all the needs arising from different motivational states will have equivalent impact on the results drive. 'Sympathy', either directed at self or others, although important for team working, will not be as results-oriented as other states such as 'Seriousness' or 'Mastery'.).

One thing is certain – there must be openness about individual needs and a willingness to give and receive support for each other's goals. Secondly, this openness needs to be framed in terms of the support that individuals can expect to receive in pursuit of their goals within the terms of the task, and from within the wider resources of the group, ie the connectedness process should deal not just with the rewards an individual can get from co-operating on the task but from belonging to the team itself – in other words the developmental potential of the team.

In delivering their outputs, enterprising teams will need to be well connected both within and outside the organization. Creating this network will allow the energy of resources, information, understanding and support to flow into the team and the outputs of the team to be accepted and not resisted. Every team member's network needs mobilizing and integrating in support of this cause. This connectedness will also enhance the team's ability to spot where they can gain quick wins. Teams that can respond opportunistically are going to have advantage over those who burn up energy missing the obvious.

This last point highlights a critical aspect of entrepreneurial finish missing in many teams. Teams need not just awareness, but also the processes for dealing with opportunities AND risks. It is still rare to find a team that systematically identifies, monitors and has strategies for risk. Yet this is the key not just to survival today but also to learning itself. Teams need to develop a view of all the links in the system in which they work and how chains of cause and effect might run. Such a view will help them identify not only opportunities and threats but also to understand how they can really influence their destiny.

TEAM MEMBERSHIP

So, what is to be expected from team members in producing these high-energy team climates? As discussed in the previous chapter, we may need to challenge our assumptions about this. Summarizing the arguments so far, the following seem to be driving changes in our perspectives on how to develop and utilize teams. Firstly, they often have to discover for themselves new ways of working, as both the goals and circumstances in which they are working will be novel. Secondly, team members will often find themselves members of more than one team, with different needs and objectives. The team will be made up of full-time and part-time members. Lastly, the membership of such teams is often characterized by high levels of turnover, with new members constantly joining and others leaving.

Quite a lot of what is written about teams has looked at the different roles that team members can play. There are two sorts of roles – functional and process. Functional roles define the contribution an individual can make to a task and are usually derived from specialist experience and knowledge, eg finance or marketing. Process roles concern the way individuals combine to achieve the desired levels of performance through contributing to the way the team works in pursuit of its objectives. They are popularly known through the works of such researchers as Belbin and his 'team role categorization'.

Functional roles

It is obviously important that a team has the right mix of experience and skills to succeed, but a number of problems might occur if we establish teams on the basis of a number of functional roles. What if someone is already competent in more than one functional area – is it necessary to include someone else? It may be politically expedient but is it efficient? What if the end result is that you have too many people on the team, with relatively little involvement, just so you can cover all the functional angles? Crazy though it sounds, it is not unusual to find team meetings held involving people with little to contribute, but there to ensure functional representation. (While accepting the importance of cross-functional communication there must be other ways of achieving this.) On the other hand, what if there are simply not enough people available to ensure the selection of teams on a role-functional basis – do you cancel the team or call in the consultants?

Perhaps a more serious problem in selecting teams on a functional role basis is that the problems and challenges often facing teams do not neatly break down into the discrete parcels of different functional perspectives. It is the nature of real world challenges that they are messy and unruly and what is really required are problem-solving/decision-making skills and sophisticated personal and interpersonal skills that can integrate these different perspectives, seeing the implications of the differences in the perspectives. Often, understanding what needs to be done is more about seeing the problems that lie in the gaps in the functional pavement, as it were. This after all is part of the purpose of creating teams.

It should not be assumed that selecting team members from across different functions produces a cross-functional perspective. It is much safer to start with the talents and skills of different individuals and in particular their ability to think integratively, and apply these to an analysis of the task the team faces. Organizations need to matrix individual talents to team requirements and ensure that the functional angles are adequately covered. A focused team, managing itself properly, will get the functional underpinning it needs either from its members or by seeking it from outside when required.

Process roles

While the work on process roles has been valuable in highlighting the importance of considering the contributions that need to be made to the successful enactment of process in teams, they too have limits to their usefulness in understanding what a successful team needs to be attending to. Analysis of individuals in terms of process role contribution usually results in a person being labelled as contributing strongly in one or two roles. While this may be appropriate for largish and fairly stable teams, in other cases such labelling can be less useful. For example, how do they apply to small teams where the number of roles each person has to fill exceeds two? Also, are these roles more about describing what might happen when all the team meet together? The truth about many modern organizations is that endless meetings with all team members present are neither possible nor desirable. We need to understand much more about what it takes to be a member of a team which rarely meets as a whole but relies for effectiveness on the ability of smaller sub-groups or even individuals to act on its behalf in a collectively responsible way. I would argue that the circumstances in which many teams will increasingly find themselves, where high levels of change and operating from dispersed locations result in fewer face-to-face contacts, mean that the concept of teams consisting of people with fixed roles and contributions, being able to practice and develop to acceptable performance levels over time, may not be appropriate.

Team contributions

For all these reasons it is probably more useful to think of team membership in terms of the differing contributions individuals can make. What will be required will be team members, and in particular team leaders, who can see the differing contribution needs of particular teams and adapt their behaviour accordingly. Reversal Theory, in recognizing that people are essentially dynamic in terms of how they feel and act, suggests that we may well be more potentially flexible and able to respond to this challenge than has so far been presumed. (However, in certain circumstances this would be extremely difficult to achieve successfully.) The aim should be to develop motivational versatility and behavioural skills so that team members can access different ways of contributing, extending their repertoire of ways in which they can add and gain energy from a team.

By acknowledging the different ways people can be motivated in relation to team membership, it is possible to clarify and develop the skills that will build high-energy teams. Developing the idea of a dynamic framework of motivational states, it is therefore possible to suggest the following areas of contribution that will combine to create a high-energy team.

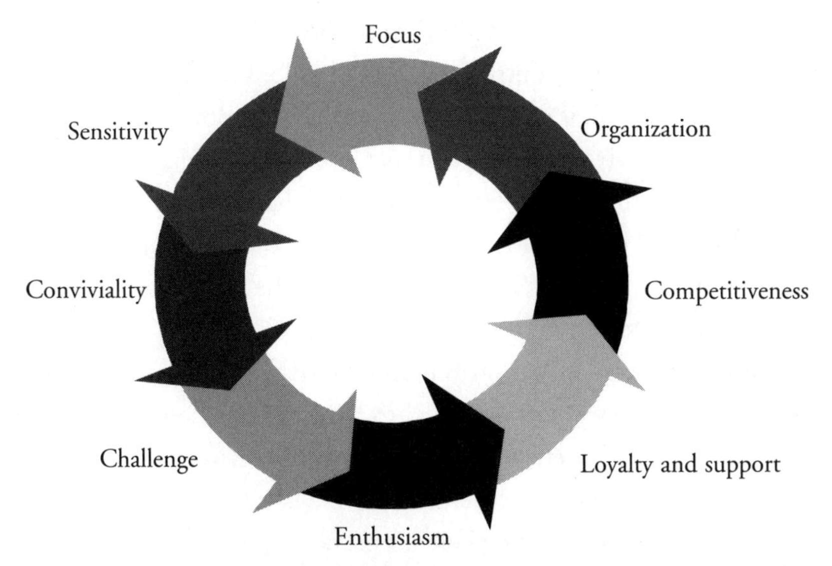

Fig. 10.2 The team contribution model

Based upon the motivational states or combinations of them (eg Self and Mastery = Competitiveness; Other and Sympathy = Loyalty and Support), there are eight ways in which individuals can contribute to building a Renaissance team:

1. **Focus** – helping to establish and maintain a vision and goals for what it wants to achieve and encouraging the team to relate its tasks, plans and activities towards those goals. Contributors are also keen that there are clear criteria for progress towards those goals and that these are monitored.
2. **Enthusiasm** – this is about committing energy and a sense of excitement to a team, encouraging it to take risks and experiment: bringing a sense of fun. Contributors want the team to stretch itself to the full. Contribution here releases excitement and ideas.
3. **Organization** – by being concerned that a team follows sensible rules and procedures which everyone agrees to. Encouraging the team to follow an acceptable way of doing things, which may have its origins either within the team or through the team being part of a wider organization. This contribution includes a sense of obligation to agreed goals and ways of doing things. Contributors want to resist unnecessary conflict that might disrupt the efficiency of the group.
4. **Challenge** – this is a contribution that questions both what the team is doing and how it is doing it. Someone may contribute here by playing the 'devil's advocate', or at a deeper level he or she may profoundly disagree with some of the assumptions that have been made. Such a contribution helps to overcome 'group think' and is an important contribution to change. This contribution is the basis of creative conflict highlighted above.
5. **Competitiveness** – this contribution is based upon an individual harnessing his/her own personal need to win, or be in control, or learn for the needs or benefit of the team (it would relate most closely to the needs for achievement identified in the BASIS data).
6. **Conviviality** – contributing here means being friendly and interested in maintaining good relationships with team members. A contribution here 'oils the social wheels' of the team.
7. **Loyalty and support** – this is the contribution that does most to develop team spirit. People seek to make sure that they do everything

they can to help the team succeed. One way this might be expressed is through offering assistance and perhaps coaching to other team members. Alternatively, trusting others and building trust. Being concerned to help others to shine.

8. **Sensitivity and reassurance** – protecting people's feelings and making sure that their emotional and personal needs are understood. Encouraging respect for the views and perspectives of others.

The final two contributions are the basis for creating the open, safe and supportive environment that allows people to challenge and question – the result of which is a team that can learn and innovate. Many of these contributions would be recognized by workers at the Opel Eisenach factory discussed earlier, where friendship, belonging and team pride are emphasized alongside challenge, responsibility and control.[6] (Team members can, on their own initiative, stop the production line if they feel it is necessary.)

Every one of these contributions is aimed at meeting different motivational needs or combinations of motivational needs. Interestingly, individuals contribute in this way because of their own needs, not necessarily those of others or the team. Even loyalty and support is about 'my need to meet your need'. It therefore does not necessarily mean that these needs are met in ways that lead to a productive team climate. Sometimes individual's needs can be met inappropriately and can inhibit the functioning of a team, for example, a team member being overenthusiastic, overly concerned with being friendly, or personally competitive at the expense of the success of the whole (see Connections, below).

CONNECTIONS: THE TEAM CONTRIBUTION MODEL

Applying this model enables teams to analyze how they are individually and collectively contributing. Using a short questionnaire individuals rate both the extent they want and feel able to contribute across the eight areas. Using a separate questionnaire they also rate how they feel other team members contribute to or inhibit team performance. Feedback is thus available to each team member in each area of contribution on:

- How I want to contribute;
- How I feel able to contribute;
- How others in the team see me as contributing;
- Whether my contribution in this area sometimes inhibits the team;
- Effectiveness.

The feedback usually stimulates powerful reviews through which a whole range of issues can be aired and dealt with. Distinguishing between contributions that work and contributions that hinder often helps individuals to manage that subtle but important distinction, where a well-meant contribution becomes a misplaced strength!

The feedback also helps the team identify which development techniques are going to be most valuable and for whom.

BUILDING RENAISSANCE TEAMS

Following on from this, team development will be concerned with creating high levels of skill in the way individuals contribute. It seems there are only three levers to developing good quality team processes, which ideally should all be employed. You can:

- focus on the interpersonal skills of the team members;
- improve the way the team is led or managed; and
- take steps to improve the operating climate in which the team operates.

The importance of building teams with strong levels of interpersonal skills was emphasized earlier. This can either be achieved through selection or development. Selection as a tool for team-building, of course, has some limitations. There simply may not be enough of the people with the right level of task and interpersonal skills to go round. There is then the dilemma of whether someone should be selected on the basis of strong team skills and weaker task skills or vice versa. There is no hard rule for this, although the former might be a better option than has been supposed. Developing the skills is the other option, and team-building events, when well run, do seem to release or in some cases promote a much higher skill level in this area. Team development events also allow a level of psychological and informal contracting to occur between team members over how individual expectations might be met, over the way the team is going to operate, and what the vision of the team should be.

Turning back to Goleman's[7] excellent review of our understanding of what it is for someone to be emotionally and socially intelligent, then clearly we are looking for strengths almost above all others in this area. The evidence is growing that teams with higher levels of emotional intelligence will outperform those with a similar, or perhaps even higher, level of technical skill, but lower level of EQ. I would suggest that any team in which there was a reasonable representation of the skills and qualities suggested in Table 10.1, has a much greater chance of success than a team lacking them.

Table 10.1 Team membership skills

Summary of emotionally intelligent behaviours within teams:
♦ Networking;
♦ Rapport building;
♦ Trust building;
♦ Consensus building;
♦ Taking multiple perspective views;
♦ Self-reliance;
♦ Initiative taking;
♦ Persuasiveness;
♦ Role modelling;
♦ Co-operation building.

The leadership of teams in today's complex and chaotic environment – which will often result in the need for pathfinder teams – will be dealt with more fully later. Suffice it to state for the moment that such leadership will require sophisticated personal and interpersonal skills, an approach which is flexible, innovative and responsive to individual and local differences, and the power and the determination to resource a local solution. Their power will be greatly enhanced if they are able to role model the behaviours that are going to be expected of the rest of the team.

In terms of particularly entrepreneurial finish, a team may well need a sense of destiny – the belief and assumption that the team is capable of delivering its results. If a team needs to have means to deliver, then it also has to believe that it can deliver. This belief will depend partly on the individual personality of the team members, partly on the culture and behaviour of the organization to which the team belongs but also and perhaps most of all, on the leadership of the team. Again in the anecdotal literature, you can read of teams overcoming the odds despite initial low morale and very adverse circumstances through the ability of a leader to inspire, motivate and resource – emotionally, intellectually and practically.

The third lever to improve team performance is the climate or culture of the organization. This is a complex piece of organizational development in which many of the issues highlighted in this book will need to be addressed. However, a culture which emphasizes strong networking and interpersonal skills and focuses on the versatility and potential of the people within it is likely to go a long way in creating the conditions in which teams can promote their contribution.

CONNECTIONS: A CHANGE MANIFESTO

Working on a series of team development events with a variety of organizations, I have asked the teams involved to draw up a 'change manifesto' that addresses many of the issues raised in this and the previous chapters. The idea is for the team to construct a reference point for change, highlighting, among other things:

- a vision statement;
- a map of stakeholder expectations;
- identification of risk;
- protocols for decision-making, meetings etc;
- key priorities and accountabilities;
- agreements on how the team want to work together, and so on.

The value of these has been recognized in improved planning, more open discussions, a greater clarity over what the team is for and better management of key external relationships.

TEAM JOINING

Although the work of Apter, Anderson and others has helped us to establish the conditions for effective team work, the problem remains, given the ad hoc, time-limited nature of teams in many organizations and the demands on individuals for multiple team membership – how can this process be accelerated?

One way in which this might be promoted by an organization is through recognizing that teams and work groups could be drawn from a more informal, loose network of people with a wide range of job skills but with the deliberate encouragement of the sorts of skills that can be derived from emotional intelligence. This would allow the optimum grouping of skills for a particular problem, in a situation in which much of the team-building groundwork had already been done, ie the team were already on the way to developing the trust that would support their efforts. A further advantage of this approach is that the existence of this loose informal network ties the team into an extremely resourceful and flexible support – one in which functional and expert support can be drawn in whenever required. This highly adaptive approach allows the twin manifesto principles of differentiation and integration to be met. The diversity of the whole organization is available within the team in a situation in which it can be most profitably accessed, and the deliberate fostering of informal networks provides the integrating function by which this can happen. Furthermore the collective learning of the whole organization can be engaged.

Teams themselves would also benefit from agreeing for themselves how they are going to bring people on board. This should not just be for full-time members of the team but part-time members as well.

CONNECTIONS: TEAM JOINING

An issue that has arisen several times with a number of companies that I have worked with is how does a team maintain its new level of climate and way of working in times of high turnover? Working with one company over a period of time we tackled this problem head on by asking the team to create a written induction process. Those who had recently joined the team and were keenly aware of the difficulties they had faced on arrival led this. The success of this was in part demonstrated by their continued high rating on a Team Climate Inventory (the questionnaire that backs up the work of Anderson and West), despite having a 50 per cent turnover in staff over a few months. It would have been reasonable to assume with this level of turnover that areas such as vision, trust and creative conflict would have been reduced while people rebuilt the team.

SELF-MANAGED TEAMS

In the vision of Renaissance organizations described earlier, I described the possibility of organizations being made up of dynamic, self-forming teams, creating energy for the organization through innovation in terms of differentiation and efficiency. This was a vision of a possible future. Not many organizations are at a time in their evolution in which they could establish these. Most organizations, I would claim, would be in a position to seriously consider self-managing teams. Teams that can manage to achieve high-energy team climates in the way described earlier deserve to be self-managing. In Chapter 6 I argued that the demands for flexibility and responsiveness make it important for frontline teams to be in the position to take the decisions, innovate and adapt to meet local conditions as well as deliver the company strategy. If these teams are really going to be able to develop connectedness between local needs and the overall direction of the business then the need to manage themselves becomes obvious. The debate is over the extent to which the team needs to designate someone as a manager, or share the authority and responsibility among themselves. Again there will be no hard and fast rule to this, but probably the energy-efficient assumption would be the latter, rather than creating an unnecessary, and perhaps energy-suppressing role. (There may well be someone designated leader/manager but his/her role will be not one of control but more to do with connectedness, resourcing facilitation and coaching.)

CONNECTIONS: SELF-MANAGED TEAMS[8]

Most of the examples of self-managed teams have been from the manufacturing industry but increasingly they are found in other areas. The Nationwide Building Society in the UK, the country's largest mutual, has recently introduced self-management into its customer service teams. The results have been impressive:

Table 10.2 Performance of mortgage and insurance customer service teams

	February 96	February 97	April 97
Productivity (work items handled per person per day)	126	176	196
Staff numbers	184	156	154
Work items received (per week)	21,909	19,182	18,151
Work outstanding (items remaining at the end of each week)	4,565	2,653	2,305
Sickness (days per month)	114	24	27
Overtime (hours per month)	524	0	0
Turnaround (time to complete work item)	4 days	2 days	2 days
Complaints	361	216	60

REFERENCES

1. Anderson, N R and West, M A (1994) *The Team Climate Inventory*, ASE, Windsor.
2. Morgan, G (1986) *Images of Organisation*, Sage, Newbury Park, California.
3. Tjosvold, D (1991) *Team Organisation: An enduring competitive advantage*, John Wiley, Chichester.
4. Leonard, D and Straus, S (July-August 1997) Putting your company's whole brain to work, *Harvard Business Review.*
5. Nystrom, H (1990) Organisational innovation, in West, M A and Farr, J L (eds) *Innovation and Creativity at Work: Psychological and organisational strategies*, John Wiley, Chichester.
6. Haasen, A and Shea, G (1997) *A Better Place to Work*, AMA, New York.
7. Goleman, D (1996) *Emotional Intelligence*, Bloomsbury Publishing, London.
8. Scott, W and Harrison, H (October 1997) Full team ahead, *People Management*, IPD, London.

CHAPTER 11

RENAISSANCE MANAGEMENT: BRINGING IT ALL TOGETHER

CONNECTIONS: THE WAY WE WERE/THE WAY WE WILL BE?

QUESTION: What do you get if you mix the Protestant Church, the nineteenth-century Prussian military system, the invention of the water-driven weaving machine and the Californian beach?

ANSWER: Management today.

Incongruent? Yes, but organizations were a new twentieth-century feature of the history of mankind, and people had to borrow extensively to work out how to run them best. And they're still trying to work out how to do it. Much of what has been written about in this book is happening, somewhere or other. However, if we are experimenting with new ways of building organizations and working in them, we need to consider how we are going to manage them.

This book has been about the way organizations would, in many cases, benefit from achieving a high-energy relationship with its environment, coupled with a similar relationship with the individuals who contribute to it. So far, it has discussed these factors individually as well as looking at how some of the structures and processes, if put in place, will maximize the way the two can mutually reinforce each other.

The question still to be answered is, how is all this to be managed? What is it that, in the end, will connect individual action to organizational markets? It is often said that management is about achieving results through others – it is about the manager directing, co-ordinating, planning, influencing the efforts of others, rather than doing it him or herself. There is an assumption implied that this is something necessarily done by a particular person or group of people within an organization (often referred to as 'the Management'). It is useful at this stage not to immediately identify it as a process undertaken by a particular group of individuals, but to analyse it in its own right. Instead, there is benefit in reviewing and highlighting the following questions: what does management do? What is the context in which it does it, of which it must take account? And how should it best be positioned to make it most effective? Answering these questions will be both building upon and adding to all the arguments in this book so far. The final chapter will deal with the following rather vexed questions:

- Do we need managers?
- What are the management skills for a Renaissance Organization?
- What is senior management for?

Management as a human process

A key argument of Renaissance Management has been to find new ways to reconcile the twin needs of diversity/autonomy with integration/control. This has led to the suggestion that organizations need to develop the means of co-ordinating the whole and exploiting the potential of size, market-share innovations, and so on, without seeking to determine the actions of every part of the business. Renaissance Organizations will therefore be concerned with management that leads to

> *the alignment and co-ordination of individuals in such a way to enable them to make a high-value energy contribution to an organization, both to sustain that organization and to meet their own needs.*

What will be the scope of management implied by this description of the process? Summarizing the story so far, management will have to:

- develop and maintain psychological and employment contracts and a work climate that encourages diversity and individual commitment;
- establish connecting processes that encourage not only improvements in effectiveness and quality but also innovation and learning – with an emphasis on openness and feedback;
- establish work processes and structures that are energy-efficient; and
- build from these factors market alignment through strategic positioning and local adaptivity to create enough excess energy to enhance and develop the other factors.

Developing and maintaining this will need to cover a whole variety of aspects: from resource provision to motivation; from establishing clear expectations to providing development; from process improvement to strategic innovation.

Furthermore, it will also involve both maintaining the here and now and creating the future. This has sometimes been characterized as the transactional and transformational dimensions of management, respectively. Transformational management is about 'what happens next month, next year, in a new market, with a new product/service/brand', and has been seen as an activity of leaders. Transactional management is the work undertaken by managers to meet the current goals and processes of an organization. Peter Farey[1] has provided a useful model of this, which also highlights the often-discussed difference between concern for task and concern for people (see Fig. 11.1).

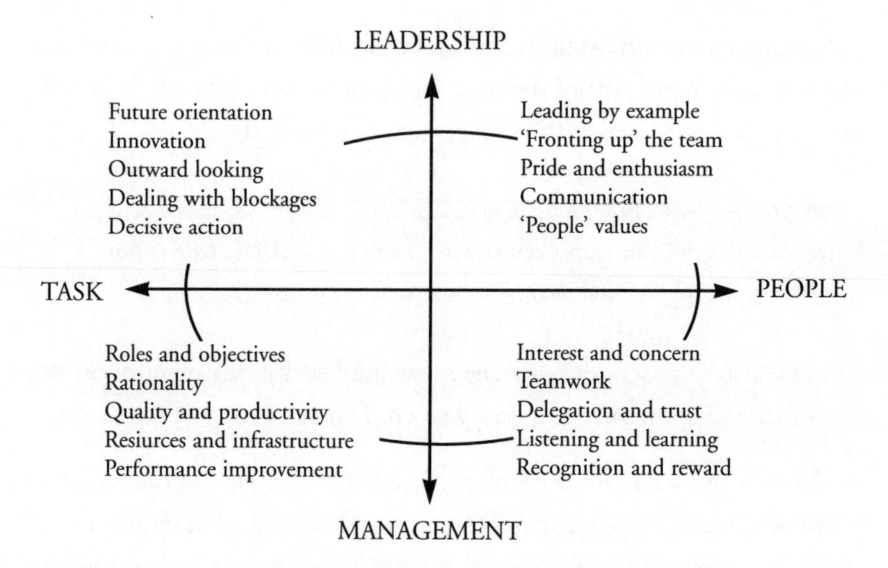

Fig. 11.1 The leadership-managership focus

The management of an organization will involve all the activities in Fig. 11.1. This does not mean that they should all be done by one person, or even that they are the prerogative of a particular job, grade or role description, although it has been supposed that this is the case. How management through leadership, and what might be called 'managership', is enacted will depend upon the way management is positioned within an organization. That, in turn, will depend upon the volatility of the market-place in which the organization is operating. It is certainly very difficult to imagine an organization that does not want management through leadership. Appreciating the reality in which it will take place will be vital. Achieving this will require much more than a rational, clinical presentation of facts, arguments and instructions; it will need a real understanding of the reality of organizations as forums for human activity.

By now it should be clear that Renaissance Organizations are those that rise to the challenge of treating people as people. One of the implications of this is that, in the arena of change that characterizes organizational life, failing to understand the human dimension to management is likely to be costly.

An organization is certainly one of the most complex systems involving human beings yet devised and, following Michael Apter's view of individuals – as essentially inconsistent and changing – it is built of further complexity. This complexity makes it very difficult to comprehend organizations in terms of how they might be managed. The reason for this is that it involves understanding and influencing the interplay between very different types of sub-system, or perhaps, more accurately, different aspects of the same complex system. The information available is too much to deal with, and so it is oversimplified to make it manageable. The problem is, however, that reality cannot be thus simplified.

A MULTI-PERSPECTIVE VIEW OF ORGANIZATIONS

Top management, probably for its own sanity, likes to assume, by and large, that it is in control but, even within a 'pocket of predictability', this control is somewhat limited. For those responsible for the future of an organization, control is usually exercised on the premise that organizations are capable of being ordered on rational principles. The assumption is that, once they have been communicated carefully to all members, proposed changes will appear self-evident and will be contested only through ignorance or stupidity. Of course, inherent in this is the view that there is a 'right' way of running an organization at a particular time, and that the top team has full knowledge of it. Managers and consultants are usually keen on analysing systems and processes in order to find more effective ways of running organizations. 'Expertise' is the authority upon which demands for change rest, and organizations are 'engineered', like machines. Relationships within this perspective are rational and instrumental; in other words, they are based on a logic that sees people fitting together to achieve a common objective.

This perspective has dominated the traditional view of organizations, but other perspectives have more recently proved valuable. Getting a grip on these other perspectives, all of which contain value and insight, is an important step towards enabling successful individual-oriented management to take place within an organization. If the traditional perspective is characterized as seeing an organization as a machine, in which the different parts of the organization work together to produce an overall result, then three other perspectives may add further to understanding (see also Fig. 11.2):

- Organizations are like families.
- Organizations are arenas for negotiation.
- Organizations are frameworks for the uneven distribution of power.

Organizations are like families

One dominant perspective in human-resource consultancy and personnel circles has been that organizations are fundamentally built on human relationships. If an organization can get those relationships right, the people involved will be better able to sort out the organization for themselves. Management is therefore about developing a positive and open atmosphere in which issues can be raised and debated, in order to promote a healthy working atmosphere. Such an atmosphere has a powerful effect on the ability of organizations to survive and thrive.

Organizations are arenas for negotiation

'Arenas for negotiation' suggests that organizations provide structures through which divergent groups of interests can negotiate for scarce resources. Each group is looking to further its interests – a development project for further funding, a planning team for extra staff, the authority to pursue a new approach. In a sense, these different groups are almost like market-places, in which different groups trade what they offer for what they want. Responsibility for ensuring positive negotiation and the aligning of different needs is a key purpose of management.

Distribution of power

An organization is also a place in which power is distributed in subtle and not-so-subtle ways. The distribution of power moves across many of the more formal structures through which an organization tries to run itself, and understanding where the power lies in an organization can be elusive. This is particularly the case when a group or individual appears to have quite minor influence at an overall level within the organization, but seems, at a local level, to have an influence far beyond its apparent status and position in the hierarchy. Power comes from all sorts of factors, from having information that others need, to controlling resources; from having a better grasp of 'how things work round here' – the power structure itself – to being associated with important initiatives; charisma may also play a part.

The distribution of power within an organization runs like fault lines through the formal structures and processes by which it tries to achieve its goals.

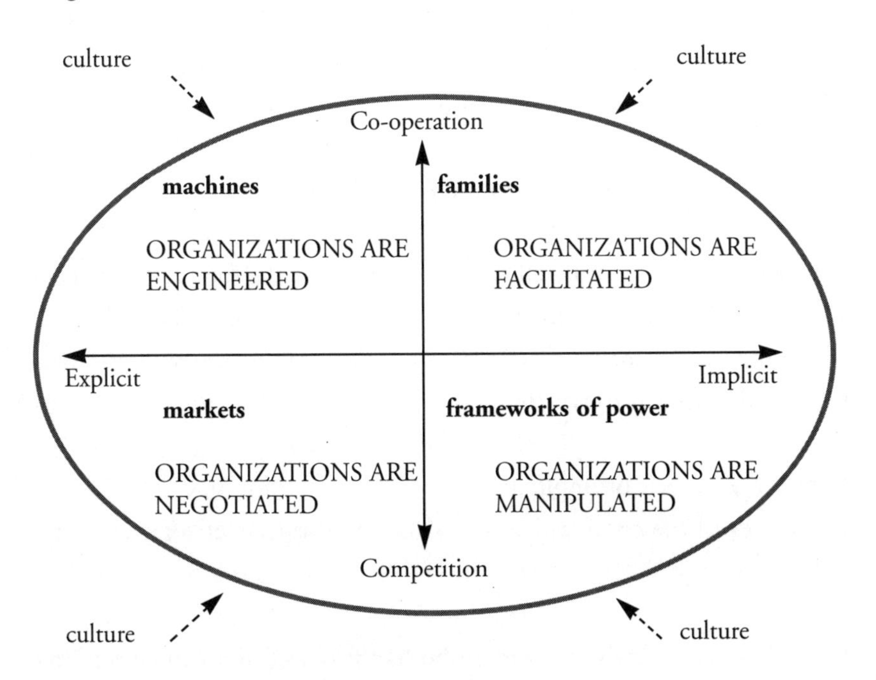

Fig. 11.2 A multi-perspective view of organizations

All four perspectives in Fig. 11.2 characterize the different ways relationships within organizations are structured and the possible ways in which they can be altered or changed. How should an organization respond to these different perspectives? Many senior managers would dismiss the families perspective as 'soft' nonsense; the power perspective may be seen as something to be denied or, if it is apparent, to be crushed, if the power does not lie with the top team. As for seeing organizations as something developed and driven through negotiation, except in the most limited sense, this is to be countered as dangerous.

While this may help a senior manager to count the hairs on his 'macho-management' chest – people with these views usually are men! – it is unlikely to take him very far in the successful management of change. It may even, as the forces characterize bigger influences in the environment, create a buffer to change in the organization. This buffer will eventually prevent the occurrence of necessary change, and it may ultimately break through, with unmanageable results.

Surely it is far better to acknowledge these perspectives and develop the skills and means to manage within them. (The skills encompassed by the term 'emotional intelligence' will be relevant from the perspectives not just of human relations but also of negotiation and power.)

The implications of managing reality

Understanding more fully all the implications of the four different perspectives will be an essential part of the understanding of the real issues facing the management of organizations. They can be characterized further, by the degrees to which

- they are explicit or implicit; or
- they reveal the competitive or collaborative aspects of organizational life.

Both these characteristics need to be handled well if an organization's responses to the forces for change are to be effective.

Explicit perspectives are engineering and negotiating relationships. The systems and structures they represent are usually quite easy to uncover, if not to respond to. Implicit perspectives, family- and power-based, are much harder to uncover, and also to deal with. In many organizations, power relationships are deep-rooted and virtually non-discussible, which is why many organizations and their managers avoid dealing with them. Consequently, power perspectives and the resulting implications for the management of organizations have been little investigated to date. Yet, according to Maestenbroek,[2] upon whose work this analysis is based, issues revealed through a power perspective contain the most influential internal forces shaping an organization:

> *A great deal of behaviour in organizations can very well be explained from power relations. Power relations can impede organizational change and adaptation more than can socio-emotional frictions or a lack of instrumental expertise.*

The heart of understanding the complexity of organizations, and seeing how to build a structure that can change to meet the conditions of a complex market, will have to be a mapping of the linkages within all four relationship perspectives. Therefore, that which has previously been unsaid needs to be acknowledged and discussed. There is nothing esoteric in this approach; it could bring greater insight into some very practical questions. For example, it could lead to the following considerations in a particular organization:

> *How will changes in the supply chain affect the ability of production to influence marketing?*
> *How is it possible to get different business units in the group to co-operate, and to act independently?*
> *How does the low morale of R&D, which has just suffered some serious disappointments, affect the organization's ability to launch new products later in the year?*

And so on…

Co-operation and competition

The second characteristic of the four-perspective model highlights whether the relationships within them are seen essentially as based on competition or co-operation. The machine- and family-based perspectives both emphasize collaborative relationships, whereas market and power relationships emphasize that organizations can be built out of competition. It is hard to imagine an organization that is free of competition, or one that is wholly built of collaborative relationships. The scarcity of resources means that there must be competition between different interest groups for resources, go-aheads and airtime. Competition is the forum through which new ideas can be tested and made to argue for their right to exist. Yet competition can be played down, and avoided, unless it degenerates into destructive conflict.

However, an organization should not promote destructive conflict, but conflict that takes place in an atmosphere of co-operation – within the context of a mutual or overarching mission or goal. In addition, co-operation is not a matter of compromise, but a case of deliberately setting out to create advantage for the other party as well as for oneself. The

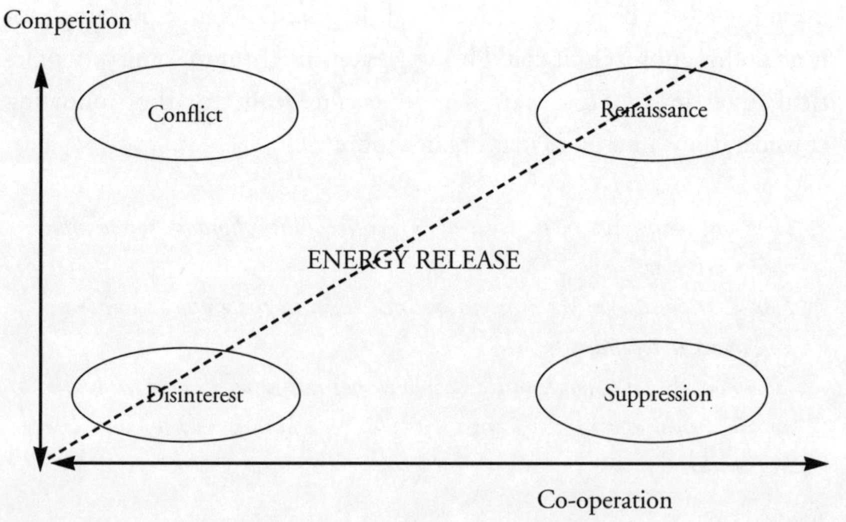

Fig. 11.3 Productive release of energy within an organization

reality of organizational life is not just that there is co-operation and competition, but that there must be. The goal for an organization must be to find the most productive way of handling both. In handling both successfully, an organization can gain the flow and energy to meet the challenges it faces; the result is true collaboration. As indicated in Fig. 11.3, one without the other will waste energy. Pure competition without co-operation will mean that energy within an organization will be wasted on internal struggles, co-operation that denies competition will lead to energy being suppressed, avoiding the reality that there must be winners and losers where there are limited resources.

POSITIONING MANAGEMENT

Given the need to manage the complexity outlined above, how should management be positioned within a Renaissance Organization? This is important – not only must the management processes take account of the 'non-mechanistic realities' of organizational life, but also of the radical shifts in relationships that are required if organizations are to develop a higher-energy environment. One way of addressing the question is to ask whether 'top-down' or 'bottom-up' management is required; this dilemma reflects the tension between control and autonomy.

Top-down management sees strategy, direction and the management of change as the key responsibility of top managers, who will decide what has to be done and cascade it down through the organization. The bottom-up view is that the only people who can really know what has to be done are those most closely connected with the actual process, and that these should be empowered to make the necessary decisions and take the necessary initiatives. In the first case, managers are the brains of the organization, clarifying direction and moving things forward. In the second, they are more like resource-providers, encouraging the innovative and adaptive actions of the front line. It might be argued that top-down management works when market conditions are stable, and demonstrate a level of predictability that encourages planning and control. Bottom-up management, it is said, is a more appropriate response to a volatility that makes rapid response and flexibility a vital part of survival and growth. The truth is that the ideal solution lies in combining the two.

Limitations to top-down responses to change

It is important to be absolutely clear about the problems that may occur with a top-down approach to management in the operating conditions in which most (but not all) organizations find themselves today. Managers in many organizations cling resolutely to the belief that, in responding to changes in the market, they can tackle them in ways that are predictable, controllable, and capable of being tackled in stages. King and Anderson[3] have called this the 'illusion of manageability'. In examining how organizations can successfully innovate, they have attacked the views, current in many popular management texts, that change is something that can be controlled by top-management design. In particular, they highlight the unpredictability of any change process, and the belief that the final outcome relies on the competence and skill of those directing the change. They argue that this illusion of manageability is composed of three component beliefs:

- the illusion of linearity;
- the illusion of predictability; and
- the illusion of control.

The illusion of linearity is the assertion that change occurs in a formal set of stages. Change is much more likely to occur through an array of parallel events, some of which advance the process, and some of which turn out to be blind alleys or wrong turnings. Change can be also be characterized by new plans being drawn at all stages, reacting to unforeseen forces and issues. This is related to the illusion of predictability already discussed here. Without predictability, there is considerable danger in using someone else's template for change. The illusion of control highlights the limited influence that senior management can have on the final outcomes of a change initiative.

Organizations need management processes that do not require local responses to be stage-managed by top managers. These managers often have neither the information, nor the control to direct a process that involves parallel processes, complexity and uncertainty.

In many ways, the illusion that senior managers can deliver is derived from the limited perspective taken by those managers who focus on a purely instrumental view of organizations. Undoubtedly, if they were able to view their organization in terms of the social, negotiated and power issues that comprise the total system, they would be in a better position to anticipate the direction and likely outcomes of change. While their control over the situation of change may still be limited, it will probably throw up fewer surprises.

Top-down management, therefore, is not a good process for maximizing the impact of change. Even worse, as strategy cannot be set other than in general terms, management's ability to direct the implementation of strategy must be recognized as limited.

Bottom-up responses – a real alternative?

To an extent, organizations will always try locally to adapt. The front line of a business, or other organization, in the absence of direction or changes coming from above, will try to adapt itself to what it sees as the imperatives for the change it is facing. This will often happen at a local level, where a particular function or business unit will create a local response to meet change forces – for example, changing products to meet local demands, using alternative suppliers, innovating in the roles they undertake, ignoring formal processes, and so on. (This is probably an example of the self-organization, outlined earlier, that occurs in any complex system trying to adapt to its environment.) Such behaviour is extremely adaptive and useful. Without this responsiveness, organizations would simply break under the strain of trying to keep up, at the formal level, with what is going on. Allowing teams to be self-managing is really a formal recognition of this impulse. Traditionally, such initiatives are usually stamped on as soon as they are discovered or, in fear of this, hidden from senior management. The unwillingness of organizations to acknowledge this is one of the reasons that political and power-based relationships start to develop. (Not the only reason of course – there are other, less organizationally focused ones!)

The problem with self-management, when it is left to emerge naturally within organizations, is that it can become incoherent from the perspective of the whole organization. In the same way, local efficiencies and effectiveness may well become inefficient and ineffective when seen in the context of the whole. The result of this is that, while local short-term health may be achieved, the whole organization will become progressively less adaptive. This is because more and more energy goes into co-ordinating the variety of responses made, leaving less and less available for dealing with the external world. For example, strategic positioning, and brand or organization identity can suffer and become fragmented.

Matrix management and cross-functional teams may provide local adaptivity and flexibility. However, unless they are structured well, they also seem to require endless meetings, a plethora of e-mail correspondence and extensive and difficult co-ordination of diaries; these are precisely the type of energy-sapping activities that Renaissance Management is trying to avoid.

BOTH/AND = RENAISSANCE MANAGEMENT

In Chapter 6, it was emphasized that successful organizational design must allow the organization to respond as a whole to the adaptive signals that emerge from those most closely in contact with the forces acting on the organization. This will occur neither in the strategic back room of an organization, nor at a purely local level. Local adaptivity should be encouraged, but it should happen in such a way that the lessons for the organization can be learned, and organization-wide responses made, where appropriate. Management should be aimed at the achievement of synergy – maximizing learning, innovation and responsiveness across the business. The value that management adds can be measured in terms of its ability to exploit scale and innovation.

Management is therefore not just about developing top-down or bottom-up decision-making; leadership and managership need to exist, not at any particular point of an organization, but in and between everything. One route to achieving this is to be very clear about the type of decisions that need to be taken within any part of the organization. In terms of the overall supply-chain process, all decisions should be made as close to the front line as possible, unless a good energy-maximizing reason can be found for acting otherwise. It is important that self-managing teams should be clear about the areas in which they can take decisions, and that the control over resources reflects this. Support activities also need to have established protocols on decision-making, which relate directly to their agreed contribution to the core business process. In addition, the connecting processes and structures need to include agreements on how decisions will be made; this will help management and leadership to maintain and enhance the virtuous energy cycle that should be its ultimate goal.

The management of Renaissance Organizations needs therefore to make explicit the levels – or types of decision-making – that belong to different parts of an organization. An example of this thinking through decision-making can be seen in Unilever, which has replaced 17 old job classes with six work levels. Their specific aim was to ensure that job-holders 'took decisions that could not be taken at lower level – and need not be taken at a higher one'. This was based upon three fundamental principles:

- all major tasks of a job fall within a single work level;
- at each higher work level, decisions taken require a broader view, involve more complexity, need more time to assess impact, and require more discretion;

- there should be only level of management in each work level.[4]

These may not necessarily be appropriate criteria for every organization, but it is important for all organizations to establish some way of defining decision-making responsibilities. The definition should take account both of local needs and of strategic direction.

From a management point of view, it might be helpful to envisage an organization as a hub, rather than as the pyramid, inverted or otherwise, that is usually used to represent it (see Fig. 11.4). This will break down the common perception that important decisions are only made by top management – 'up' and 'down' may be associated with important and unimportant. Some decisions in some organizations may be so important that everyone needs to be involved. Different organizations will no doubt create decision-making structures that include front-line staff with greater or lesser levels of influence. Not all organizations may wish to work in the same way as advertising agency St Luke's (see below), but the example of this company may help another to disentangle its own status/hierarchy and decision-making.

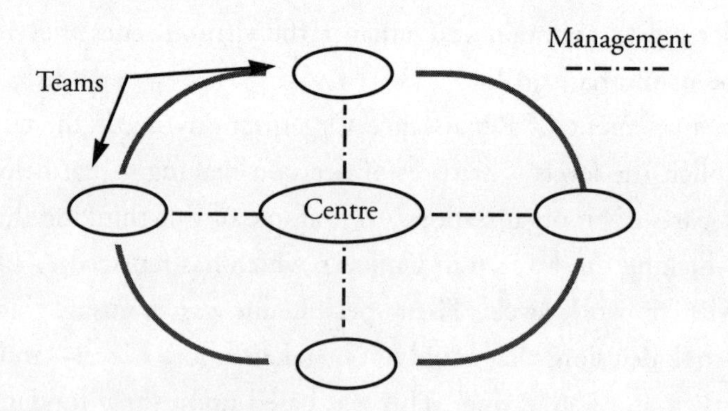

Fig. 11.4 The organization as a hub

Fig. 11.4 is not intended to represent the structure of an organization. Instead, it emphasizes the fact that the management system of an organization needs to be connected with everyone taking responsibility for playing a part in the managership and leadership of that organization. It can be used as the basis for plotting different types of decisions and establishing agreements on how this should happen. For example, how do two or more teams take a decision together? Must a decision always involve the centre, and to what extent? What communication needs to take place in these instances? Are there any decisions that must be taken by all the constituent parts, or does the centre always take decisions on behalf of the whole organization?

CONNECTIONS: ORGANIZATIONAL COMMUNISM?

St Luke's advertising agency was voted Agency of the Year by the industry magazine *Campaign.* Everyone at the agency, including the Chief Operating Officer, practises 'hot-desking'; no one has their own assigned desk, but finds one that is available or close to where they want to work on a particular day. It is a place where senior management see themselves as a service to the rest of the organization and where more junior members of staff have 'put their collective foot down when workloads were getting too heavy'. It is a company where staff appraisal of the COO and chairman is posted without censorship in the reception area for maximum visibility and share ownership depends on length of service not seniority.

'People have called what we are doing "Communism",' says David Abraham, COO, 'but we believe it is a liberation of people to pursue their own passionate ideas which will make people more productive.'[5]

SUMMARY

This analysis serves to emphasize the fact that organizations are arenas of human interaction. Renaissance Management must deal with this reality, rather than taking the more simplistic view, which is that individuals are 'cogs in a machine'. For these reasons, management cannot be replaced by a management information system allowing teams and individuals to relate to the whole purely through the PC on their desktop. It is, and will remain, an essentially human process, albeit one that can be supported by technology.

What does this mean in practice? Within organizations, this particular debate seems far less advanced than the others. There are cases of managers being encouraged to take a more coaching, facilitative style, of whole layers of management being removed, and of the need for a more 'empowering approach'. However, the management role still seems to be over-focused on hierarchy and position, and on its contribution in linking top with bottom, and being part of a command structure, even if that structure is an enlightened one. Bottom-up approaches at best often seem limited in scope, focusing primarily on process improvements. (Although within group structures high levels of autonomy can exist at business unit level, the internal structure of these business units can remain quite rigidly hierarchical and top-down.) Organizations that want to be truly high-energy will have to take a more complex view than this, and be clearer about the role of the managers they employ.

References

1. Farey, P (1993) Mapping the leader/manager: management education and development, *Association for Management Education and Development*, London, **24** (2).
2. Maestenbroek, W F G (1993) *Conflict Management and Organization Development*, John Wiley & Sons, Chichester.
3. King, N and Anderson, N (1995) *Innovation and Change in Organizations*, Routledge, London.
4. Trapp, R (March/April 1998) Unilever's global reach, *Human Resources.*
5. Jebb, F (August 1998) Don't call me sir, *Management Today.*

CHAPTER 12

THE RENAISSANCE MANAGER'S ROLE

ARE MANAGERS NEEDED?

MANAGEMENT is needed, not only in a particular part of the organization, but at all levels, from the management of self upwards. Setting aside for a moment the fact that not all organizations will want or need to move towards self-management, the simple fact that it is possible sets up an interesting challenge for the continuation of the specific role of a manager. In theory, it could be argued that the members of self-managed teams can all play a part in contributing to the leadership and managership of their team, removing the need for a specified 'team manager or leader'. Perhaps, at organizational level, information technology and a few charismatic leaders could provide, with specialist help, the co-ordination of leadership or managership required. So, what is the point of managers? Are they a doomed breed? Interestingly, society does not think so, and apparently anticipates a rise in the number of managers in the UK of over 500,000. (This is perhaps more to do with the fact that organizational thinking has not yet caught up with organizational reality, rather than evidence of a market-driven need for more managers.)

It is not yet time to write the manager's obituary notice. For a suggestion of the reasons why, see Connections, below. There is a symbolic aspect to management, and the best managers represent what the organization is trying to achieve, not just in terms of strategic objectives but also in terms of its values or what it stands for. Also apparent is the importance of relationship-building; this is clearly highlighted in the way that valued managers go about their work. Relationship-building involves treating people as individuals, seeking to enhance their contribution through a focus not just on their skills, but also on their behaviour and perspective. When individuals are acknowledged by their managers, they feel that they are in touch with power and influence, and that they have a route to getting heard. Couple these thoughts with the importance of establishing, at an individual level, a new psychological contract, and the need for management to exist between different parts of the business, and it is possible to identify a real need for managers. These are roles that cannot be carried out by PCs and charismatic leaders. Managers allow organizations to take account of the organizational reality captured in all four perspectives of an organization. They facilitate the best possible contribution from individuals and really maintain market alignment.

There will be a role for managers, therefore, although there probably will be a need for far fewer of them, and management will be seen as less of a career in itself. It will be a heavily reconstituted role, requiring a radical shift in perspective. A team potentially still needs a manager, but, although the manager may be the catalyst for successful management and leadership, he or she will not be the total embodiment of it. The role will be rarely to direct, but more often to connect. Managers will be expected to facilitate the human aspects of connectedness – not just with teams and senior managers, but also with their peers – to share good practice, influence strategy, and create a motivational and learning environment.

These emerging expectations, outlined in more detail below, will add considerable value to what a manager can bring to an organization. This will be the case whether or not the organization has fully committed itself to self-managed teams, or to team-working in general.

Connections: managers talking

Over a number of years I ran a series of week-long seminars for general managers in the UK. They were usually very senior people, drawn from a wide variety of organizations. At the start of the week we would explore their own experiences of managers they had rated highly. The results were fascinating in their consistency. Technical ability of any kind was very rarely identified as significant. When the delegates were asked to identify what makes a good manager good, the answer was almost invariably to do with the manager's interpersonal skills, and the words used were often energy-based: 'enthusiastic', 'empowering', 'inspiring'. In addition, managers typically gained personal credibility for being 'tough', 'open', 'decisive', and 'having vision and sharing it'. Being a good manager, it seemed, was more about transmitting information and resources than about having technical ability. I recorded a number of other phrases that seemed to capture this spirit:

- 'hands-on hands-off';
- 'sense of what's right';
- 'role model';
- 'the oil in the gears';
- 'integrity, credibility, belief';
- 'catch people doing things right';
- 'expectations clear in both parties';
- 'great communicator';
- 'in touch with the whole business';
- 'challenges sloppy thinking'; and
- 'sets high standards for himself and others'.

Aligning behaviours

Managers in Renaissance Organization will be there to promote leadership and managership throughout the organization, but do not necessarily have to embody themselves totally. The question that remains is, 'How does a manager conceive and undertake this expectation?' To be effective, a manager will need to take a broad enough perspective. The Renaissance manager will have the cognitive skills to see his or her organization, and the market-place and environment in which it operates, as a system. A fundamental tenet of this perspective is that the behaviours of others whom the Renaissance manager is trying to influence will be determined by this system. This is not as abstract a concept as it might sound. People are driven to behave in the way that they do, not just through personality, needs and desires but also through the expectations that others have of them. The quartermaster ruthlessly accounts for every single item that leaves the army stores because he will be punished if items are not where they are supposed to be. The bank manager is cautious and careful because he is expected to be; his superiors would not thank him for being an innovative, but cavalier, risk-taker.

In the end, people tend to do those things that they feel, either positively or negatively, are required of them. Each person justifies his or her actions by claiming that they are largely a result of the circumstances or system in which he or she works. However, this balanced view is rarely applied to the actions of others; their behaviour is explained in terms of their personality, their lack of understanding, and their perceived wilfulness. A Renaissance manager cannot view a situation in this way. In facilitating connectedness in an organization, he or she must look below the surface behaviours and perceptions to untangle exactly what needs to be done to improve energy flow. What does this mean for the skills and behaviours of the Renaissance manager? Emotional intelligence is important to individuals in general, but for managers it is essential.

However, understanding, either cognitively or emotionally, will not be enough. Organizations may be very different in the future – there will be an increase in boundary-less behaviour, and in the use of self-managed teams; and there will be a high rate of innovation, not just in what the organization is and does, but also in the way individuals create and define their own contribution. It will not be enough for managers simply to understand the complexity of the organizational system. What will be required is the ability to do something about it!

Renaissance managers will only be able effectively to help organizations balance differentiation and autonomy with integration and alignment if they develop the right new skills and behaviours. These will be very different from the traditional managerial skills, but they will not seem as radical today as they would have ten years ago. The following would certainly be important skills and behaviours for a Renaissance manager:

- mentoring;
- negotiating;
- contracting;
- energy management;
- role-modelling;
- catalysing strategy.

MENTORING

One of the key skill areas will relate to mentoring. These skills go much further than those implied by the term coaching. Although the two terms have come to mean the same thing, mentoring is actually a much wider concept that includes coaching, and other skills. The confusion is a recent one, and probably arises from the needs of trainers and consultants to offer a more sophisticated way of engaging managers in some basic skill development. Mentoring in the old days was about a senior person within an organization taking a younger colleague under his or her wing, and seeking to develop, not just some job skills, but also an idea of 'how things are done round here'. It was a sort of introduction to the company's culture and the political 'ropes'. (This was a good example of managers acknowledging the reality of organizational life before theorists did.)

Mentoring in a Renaissance Organization is about transmitting the culture and values of the organization to teams and individuals, as well as developing the technical and interpersonal skills of an individual. It is about developing people, not just on a one-to-one skill-coaching basis, but also through providing resources and opportunity so that people can manage their own development. Renaissance managers use their skills and experience to facilitate the development of individuals and teams within the context of the organization. They seek to create alignment between individuals and organizations, not to produce some ideal of 'corporate man or woman', but to create the circumstances in which each can benefit from the richness and diversity of the other, in order to enhance the learning of both. Mentoring is the means by which good practice will be shared. It should not be seen as happening just on a one-to-one basis, but should also occur with groups of people and teams. It is an ongoing and extremely visible role.

CONNECTIONS: THE FOUR BASES OF MENTORING

In the mid-1990s, I was involved in some ongoing work on the identification of good mentors in organizations.[1] The focus of the work was based on analysing the factors that individuals had found to be important in the help they had received from other managers in their development. The results suggested that there were four bases to the way that managers could help others develop:

- a positional or organizational basis suggested that help could be offered through access to information, resources, or even through the raising of an individual's profile, so that he or she was noticed by others;
- the interpersonal basis suggested that managers who were perceived as good at developing others were good listeners, accessible, tended to meet others as equals and did not try to over-control;

- on the developmental basis, some managers seemed instinctively to recognize a good learning experience, and could construct valuable learning experiences; they were natural coaches;
- the context basis was a more subtle one – some managers seemed to know why they were mentoring someone, either formally or informally. They had a specific purpose and a practical view of what was involved.

Not all successful mentoring managers had strengths in all these areas, but evident strengths in some of them were found to be helpful.

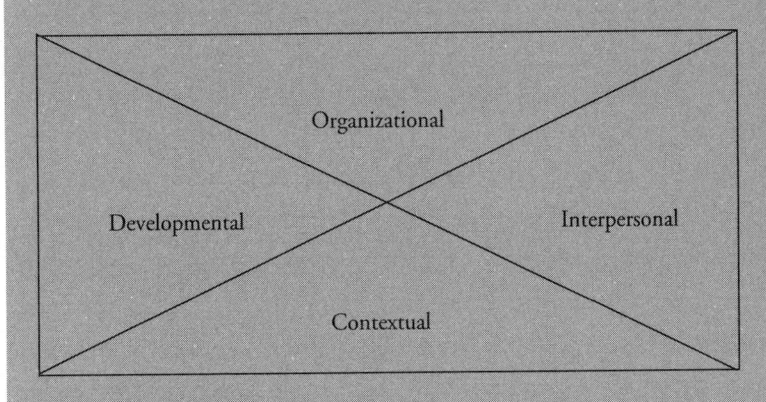

Fig. 12.1 Four bases of mentoring

NEGOTIATION

Fig. 12.2 suggests that the need to negotiate will become a more critical part of the manager's tool kit, the more volatile his or her organization finds its market-place. The move away from hierarchical control to more autonomous activity means that apparently conflicting priorities will often need to be reconciled. For example, the activities of one team will often require the support and commitment of another, but such support and commitment may not be reflected in the second team's own priorities. In the past, organizations will have taken care of this by creating a formal structure of responsibilities and procedures (but even then, as has been said, people negotiated and found 'unofficial' but effective ways of co-operating). Today, this is not possible. Teams and individuals need to work out at a local level exactly how to integrate their activities and support each other. Teams and individuals often underestimate the need for negotiation within an organization and, furthermore, their responsibility for it. Examples of this often occur within matrix structures where cross-functional teams may have to negotiate with functional teams over who does what, and how their efforts should integrate. Still working within the perspective of 'senior management knows best', and believing that there is a master plan, they fail to realize the responsibility they have to sort things out at a local level. The key skill for this will be that of win/win negotiation based upon establishing the needs of *both* parties. If managers are not directly undertaking this (on the basis of their responsibility for alignment, they should at least be involved), they should at least be encouraging effective negotiation based upon the alignment of needs in others. In ensuring effective negotiation, managers are promoting not just the needs of both parties, but also the needs of the organization as a whole. They will be able to do this, because their activity and perspective will not only focus on local activity but also on a wider perspective (see Fig. 12.2, for a catalyst for strategy).

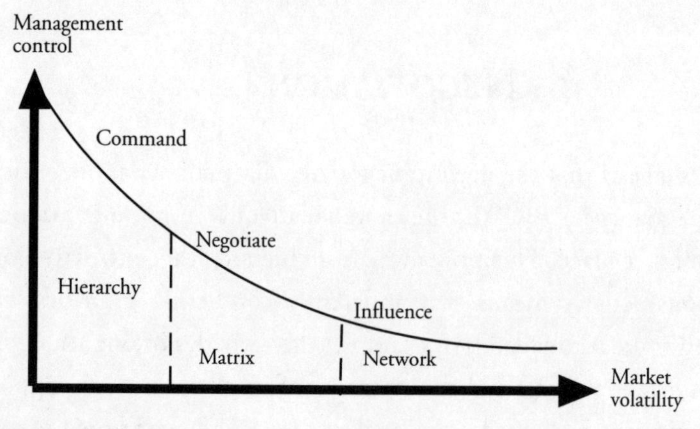

Fig. 12.2 Management control and market volatility

CONTRACTING

Contracting is related to negotiation. In their new role, managers will also need to be skilful at facilitating informal contracts at a number of levels (summarized in Table 12.1). Their ability to develop these contracts will depend not just upon a particular set of interpersonal skills, but also on their ability to resource those agreements in which they have been involved. To do this, they will need the backing of a good network and the ability to influence and gain the co-operation of others. Few of these agreements will be written down; through the manager's own personal behaviour, they will exist in an environment of deep trust.

Table 12.1 Levels of contracting

Individual with self	Personal development plan
Individual with employer	Psychological contract
Team with members	Team contract eg manifesto
Team with other teams	'Service level agreements' etc
Team/individual with organization	Strategy

ENERGY MANAGEMENT

Energy management has nothing to do with an organization's fuel bill! It is about maintaining high-energy contributions, either within teams or groups, or at, say, a business-unit level. It can be achieved not by a manager directing people, but through the manager having the skills to challenge process, standards and goals. An obsession with creating high-energy environments at a local level will be an important quality in Renaissance managers. They will also have the skills to develop, with the particular group of people with whom they work, performance measures that are relevant to them and to the organization. In maintaining a high-energy environment, managers will also make sure that the quality of feedback is appropriate.

Another aspect of energy management will be working to maintain the energy levels of the team. This will necessitate an understanding of motivation and group dynamics, so that appropriate intentions can be made. For example, a manager may notice when someone has become locked in a particular routine or task and can suggest ways in which that task may be re-construed to make it more interesting. Alternatively, he or she can encourage that person to review the task with their work colleagues, to see if changes can be agreed. In several organizations this is a role delivered by 'teamwork facilitators'. They can be found both in manufacturing and service industries.

These two examples demonstrate an instrumental perspective and the interpersonal perspective, respectively. Managers should also challenge if there is insufficient internal debate in the team, or if a counter-productive balance of power is starting to emerge within the group or team.

By not becoming over-involved in decision-making – and thereby doing somebody else's job for them – managers are conserving energy. They are also able to use their own energy for more useful activities, such as ensuring that the team has the resources it needs, and for catalysing strategy (see below).

ROLE-MODELLING

It has long been established that observing and copying the behaviour of another is one of the most powerful ways of learning, particularly at work. Conversely, it is enormously counter-productive for any managers, but particularly senior managers, to say one thing or espouse one value, and to say or do something else.

If managers can, through their behaviour and actions, demonstrate both the values and vision of the organization, it will be a potent force for integration. For instance, if they are seen as open and supportive, perceived to be setting themselves high standards and challenging others to do the same, the climate in which people work will start to reflect this. However, if managers are on the one hand trying to build co-operation, and then operating with an 'us-and-them mentality', people will make their own judgement about whether or not the organization means what it claims. Alignment needs to be reinforced in what managers say and do, and in the symbolic actions they take.

CATALYSING STRATEGY

Managers are not there to do other people's jobs for them. Nor, as has been argued, are they there to provide all the managership and leadership a team or a more traditional department needs. They should have enough time to focus on strategy, which is a key area of alignment.

Strategy and goals cannot be set by senior management alone. Existing inside an organization and away from the reality of the front line, they lack sufficient information to determine which strategy is the most relevant. Moreover, if the illusion of manageability is accepted, they are not in a position to implement it. They are in a position to create a forum in which decisions about strategy can be made. It is the responsibility of managers to propose strategy that responds both to local experience and to the identification of the need for radical innovation. To do this, managers need to work with each other. That is, across business, they should be able to create groupings that can analyse common experiences and insights, and make an energy-creating case to senior management. In this sense, managers can be said to be catalysing the formation of strategy. To do so, they will have to employ skills and behaviours that include creativity, networking, influencing and analysis, and will also need to be able to construct the proposals for energy/value improvement as a business case that the top team can understand.

Managers will have particular responsibility for the effective generation and implementation of innovation. A key theme for this book has been the need for innovation at all levels. Local innovation should not be within the direct control of senior management; decisions on strategic innovation must be. Unfortunately, the distinction sometimes becomes blurred, and senior management wastes energy by getting involved in the wrong way with adaptive innovation. In other words, senior managers often attempt to control what they do not understand, rather than seeking to learn from it on behalf of the organization as a whole. In doing so, they fail to divert enough energy towards seeing the big picture and recognizing when more radical innovation is required. The go-between must be the manager, who uses mentoring and role-modelling in order to nurture innovation in situations in which it is no longer enough simply to maintain the organization, and a more radical, strategy-altering alternative is required.

Few organizations or managers recognize this as a key behaviour and skills set of anyone but the most senior managers in an organization. I would argue that this is the principal way that a connection can be made over strategy.

WHAT IS SENIOR MANAGEMENT FOR?

The role of senior managers needs to be clarified. First, it is important to remember that they also have 'front-line' responsibilities, usually dealing with a number of stakeholders, including shareholders or owners. Secondly, they will probably remain the strategic decision-takers, approving goals and the allocation of resources. However, they will now do this within a much more dynamic relationship with the organization as a whole, in which strategy is often proposed by one individual or group, and the details of implementation worked out by others. Lastly, senior managers ensure that alignment and synergy are alive and well and promoted throughout the organization, so that the experience they have is available to those who need it. This will be achieved by the senior manager acting as an internal consultant who is available to support any part of the business where he or she can add value.

The senior manager's energy contribution will be enhanced if he or she maintains an active and relevant network outside the business. On the basis of pure prejudice, I believe it is high time that many senior managers took responsibility for looking outside their own organization to connect it more closely to the greater system of which it is part.

Summary

The purpose of a manager can therefore be summarized as the development of a connectedness across the business; the manager should also ensure that adequate levels of leadership and managership exist within the particular areas for which he or she is responsible. This will be an intensely human activity, requiring a deep understanding of how individuals and organizations really work. In the past, the role of managers often blocked energy flow; the new purpose of management should enhance that flow.

Connections: and because I'm a consultant...

As I finished writing this book, I was invited to speak at a conference of managers in Holland. I attempted to summarize everything under a 'Renaissance Manifesto', and I include this 'manifesto' here as an overview of this book:

- Build a business from individuals.
- Strive to be different as well as better.

- Embrace complexity and unpredictability.
- Understand your organization and markets as an energy system.
- Let those decide who can decide.
- Remember, managers connect, not direct.

Reference

1. Carter, S N (1994) *An Essential Guide to Mentoring*, Institute of Management, Corby.

INDEX